Advance Praise

New Lenses offers encouragement and advice to any parent whose adult children have been unable (or unwilling) to leave the family nest. The book doesn't promise to be a quick and easy fix to every family's challenges. It's more like a guide to self-discovery and personal growth. Read, journal, reflect, and implement the wisdom found within these pages, and discover the better life that awaits you!

—**Beverly Mattox**, *Founder & Creative Director,*
360 Digital Media

What does it take to get us moving? To propel us, finally, from paralysis to action, from the starting line to the course? Life sends us all kinds of signals but even those often fail to push us forward. Along comes a gentle but firm nudge from a friend. This is what Pam Reid is doing with *New Lenses*. She nurtures while guiding us to the next thing, the place we can almost but not quite see. She provides the focus and depth of field we need to bring the beautiful picture from our dreams into reality. Pam's book, the examples she shares with brutal honesty from her own life, the kind way she helps us see what you already know… these words are miraculously here at exactly the moment when we don't know what to do but absolutely know that another day of what you've been doing is not the answer. Read this if it's time to change. (You know it is.).

—**Joyce Beverly**, *Publisher, Fayette Woman Magazine*

New Lenses takes the reader to a pivotal pause of self-examination. The author offers a spiritual prescription filled with insight, wisdom, and personal parable. This is just what the doctor ordered! It's personal and applicable for any individual or family dealing with life's hurdles and challenges.

–FeFe Handy, *Chief Executive Director,*
Page Turners Make Great Learners

This book is an amazing little gem! It's a quick read and filled with nuggets of wisdom from one page to the next that will leave you thinking long after you have turned the last page. The author has a gift for seeing into the heart of what really matters in life and spelling out a recipe to achieve your personal best. The premise of the book is how to relate to your adult child who has not successfully moved out on his or her own, but the book is so much more than that. Pam Reid has a gift for imparting profound truths in a down home and relatable way. There were so many places in the book I wanted to underline and remember for later. An amazing compilation of life lessons you will want to keep next to your bedside and read again and again!

–Becky Davenport, *Executive Director, Bloom Our Youth*

New Lenses truly has provided a new perspective for me as a parent. The journey of success and failure of our children usually weighs heavily on our conscience as a barometer for how well we are doing as a parent. What Pam Reid provides is some clarity and reflection which will allow any parent to navigate simply by recognizing the strength in the ability to apply feeling love over worry (FLOW) despite any circumstance or challenge associated with parenting. This book is an honest and transparent discussion that needs to be had.

–Marcus L. Broadhead, *Ed.D, Educator*

When you feel like you have failed as a parent because all the hopes and dreams you had for your child seems to have taken a devastating turn, put on a fresh lens, one that reflects on you. This book gently turns the focus on you and gives the author's personal story about the years of hurt and disappointment having no place in her heart. The author's story, her "personal prescription," and resources throughout the book are invaluable. Each chapter teaches you to understand how your love, your responsiveness, and your willingness to open up to your current circumstances will heal you and those around you. The writing is simple and engaging, like a cup of tea with my favorite friend. My handy guide going forward!

–Linda L. Carter, *Project Manager – Six Sigma Specialist*

New Lenses: A Prescription to See Your Adult Children Differently is a book that will resonate with the whole family. The author's knack for writing makes the reader feel as though they are having a one-on-one conversation with the author. You will discover after reading this book that not only are her personal stories very relatable, but equally meaningful is how the author's application of steps such as "Personal Prescriptions," teaching you to "FLOW - Feel Love Over Worry", the "I am's"; how to be "Reflective and Ready" offer the reader the freedom to explore their personal goals and dreams all the while creating new lenses and learning a prescription to see their adult children differently. It's not only a game changer for parents with children of all ages, but it will certainly be time well spent. A must read.

–Tracy Skinner, *Owner, Truefig, LLC*

The author seeks to give parents of adult children living at home the tools necessary to better cope with an ever-changing landscape. The tools the author provides and the way she presents them in *New Lenses* are competent, timely, well-organized and will definitely strike an accord with any reader. Once I started reading, I could not put the book down because there were so many stories and situations that applied to what I'm dealing with currently. I learned that I too was "the enemy!" Every parent with adult children living at home must read this book...I give it a '10'!

–**Mark Tyree**, *Division Supervisor, Town of Huntington*

New Lenses is a masterfully written book that has perfectly interwoven the fabric of Pam Reid's life into an inspirational memoir that oozes with lessons on love, life, and leadership. Even though it is penned for parents it is appropriate for every man, woman, and child.

–**Hasani Pettiford**, *Author, Speaker, Pastor, Co-Founder of Couples Academy*

New Lenses

PAM REID

New Lenses

A Prescription to See Your Adult Children Differently

NEW YORK

LONDON • NASHVILLE • MELBOURNE • VANCOUVER

New Lenses

A Prescription to See Your Adult Children Differently

Published in New York, New York, by Morgan James Publishing in partnership with Difference Press. Morgan James is a trademark of Morgan James, LLC. www.MorganJamesPublishing.com

ISBN 9781642794267 paperback
ISBN 9781642794274 eBook
ISBN 9781642795288 Audio
Library of Congress Control Number: 2019930350

Cover Design by:
Christopher Kirk
www.GFSstudio.com

Interior Design by:
Chris Treccani
www.3dogcreative.net

Cover Photo by:
Pam Reid

Morgan James is a proud partner of Habitat for Humanity Peninsula and Greater Williamsburg. Partners in building since 2006.

Get involved today! Visit
MorganJamesPublishing.com/giving-back

I dedicate this book to my sister, Monique Alston, who before she lost her battle with ALS, encouraged me every step of the way. No matter what I embarked upon, she was my all-time biggest cheerleader, and I miss her terribly.

Table of Contents

Foreword

Every now and then, you may come across a book and an author, so encouraging and motivating that you go out of your way to share your find, with everyone you know. I believe that this wonderfully talented individual and her debut work, New Lenses, is that rare find. Author, speaker and business consultant, Pam Reid will take you on a journey sharing some of the most intimate moments in her life, in hopes that you too will be encouraged to fulfill your destiny. The thoughts, ideas and suggestions in this book are designed to give you clarity as you navigate life, as well as with the dynamics and challenges that may exist at home, at work, and even in your local community.

I first met Pam Reid almost a dozen years ago, and I've witnessed firsthand, how she has championed and cultivated a community of young people to believe they can achieve incredible things. Her writing style is simple, yet powerful, and carries the message that being able to FLOW (Feel Love Over Worry), is integral to achieving things one never thought imaginable. Her genuine desire for her readers is that they learn how to FLOW. That they learn how to feel love over worry; love over weakness; love over weariness; love over wrongdoing; love over whatever it is that is keeping them from living their best life.

Pam is spot on with the steps you can take to have richer, deeper, more meaningful relationships in your life. In this book you will be provoked and challenged to give thought to what may contribute to the behaviors demonstrated by those we love, as well as our own, and the impetus for the decisions that lead to the circumstances and situations people sometimes find themselves in. Be prepared. You may even find yourself reevaluating and rethinking what you're currently doing, or what you should be doing in your life journey.

As a Paralympic gold medalist, I personally know what it means to overcome insurmountable obstacles and to be the best God created me to be. In my 19 years as a Community Pastor, I see how lives can be changed when the desire for families and community has a transformative impact, and becomes a driving force to be in the center of God's will. New Lenses added to the passion I have to share my God-given gifts, and to continue to live and lead from my true purpose. I can see myself pursuing the next level of life God has planned for me.

I am honored and delighted to have an opportunity to open the door to Pam's family room, as she invites you in and speaks to you like a friend who genuinely has your best interest at heart. My hope, as you read this book, is that you open your heart to the principles and prescriptions she offers. Regardless of where you are in your own personal journey, I am convinced that New Lenses will inspire, encourage and motivate you to act. This book is packed with inspirational stories, biblical principles and anecdotes that are sure to resonate with the person whose desire is real and sustainable change . . . the person who knows that it's time!

If you are ready for a new set of lenses, with just the right prescription to see your world and the people in it differently, then this book is for you. May you be blessed, like I am, by the gift Pam Reid has to offer.

Al Mead
Paralympic Gold Medalist
Pastor of Community, New Hope Baptist Church

Background

Chapter 1:

The Narrow Road

———•—•———

"People take different roads seeking fulfillment and happiness. Just because they're not on your road doesn't mean they've gotten lost."

DALAI LAMA

don't know any parent who doesn't want the best for their children. Actually, I don't know any parent who doesn't want the best life for themselves. The parents I know and work closely with are hardworking, loving people. There isn't anything they wouldn't do for their children. Their sacrifices are sometimes excessive, and almost always are at the expense of something. I don't judge though. I can't. I've made my fair share of sacrifices and accommodations, and offered plenty of rationale and excuses for what my husband and I allowed and tolerated during the early years of raising our children. All seemed, at least at some level, to have been in balance during our children's elementary, middle, and high school years. Well, not so much during the middle and high school years. It's at the end of middle school and the beginning of high school that we saw very clear glimpses into the kind of young adults our children would become. Perhaps you saw some indication in yours, much earlier.

Suffice it to say, sometimes we recognize early on when things aren't going quite in the direction we had planned, and we're able to shift and make measurable adjustments in behavior and responses with the hope that we can steer things in a better direction. But what happens when we don't recognize that something's going awry? What do you do when you and your child are beyond the high school and college years, and you're concerned about what your child is planning to do with their life? You wonder when they are planning to transition and make good use of the college education you made countless sacrifices for them to obtain? What do you do when you wake up and realize everything has pretty much gone to, you know what, in a handbasket?

As a teenager, I remember being barely able to contain myself waiting for the day I could get my driver's license. Even more exciting would be the day I would move out of my parent's house. Get from under my parent's rule and watchful eyes. My friends and I graduated from high school and happily went our separate ways to college, university and, for some of us, work or the military. We were free to live our lives and never, and I do mean never, did we look back or even consider to return home for even a moment.

Today, 45 percent of young American adults are still living at home with parents and relatives. Experts call this family dynamic a trend, and there are a host of reasons for this shift in how adults, ages 18-34, choose to live; all of which you can search on the internet. Failure to Launch, abbreviated FTL, is the term given to describe the situation of an adult child living at home and highly dependent on parents. When these young adults are dealing with the challenges associated with anxiety and other mental disorders, the situation is exacerbated and stress runs high for everyone involved. Not all young FTL adults have mental disorders. No indeed. Some are challenged by other things like laziness, unwillingness, or immaturity. They consistently make poor choices and drain your finances, which unfortunately can put a real strain on your relationships with others. You can't help but feel like the situation is a direct reflection of you, so here comes the shame covering you like a blanket.

It's important to note that not all young adults who live at home with their parents are lazy, unwilling, or immature. Not at all. Many simply choose to live at home. I am aware of quite a few who do very well for themselves and some who make six-figure salaries. They are saving money for homes of their own, and helping out their parents while they do. Some are in transition. They have great jobs and find themselves back at home due to a divorce or other challenging life circumstance. Some are back at home because their parents need them. It could be an accident, illness, or some other emergency where the adult child rises to the occasion to help. There are some who are continuing their education well beyond their master's, and parents are happy to support and be a refuge for these young adults.

When living at home has much to do with laziness, an unwillingness, or immaturity, parents can easily find themselves feeling blindsided and trapped. This is usually coupled with feeling mentally, emotionally, and financially drained. Oh, and please let's not leave out the shame of it all. It's a tough place to be. Far too often I see the distraught look on the faces of these parents. What I hear most about in talking with these parents is their stories of shame. It pulls at my heart to see their trepidation in how they interact and engage with others, not knowing when the topic of children will come up. Some parents choose to engage less and less with others and so begin a life of isolation.

The question that causes the most physical and emotional discomfort is the one that asks how your child is doing. Folks like to brag about their children – and rightfully so! It's just hard to hear the accolades and successes of other people's children when yours has not done anything notable or made any progress since graduating from high school.

Now what about you? This constant state of dis-ease and anxiety can wreak havoc on your health and overall well-being. You've got things to do, dreams to help manifest into reality, and goals to achieve. You've got an amazing life to live. You've got experiences to enjoy and opportunities to take advantage of. Opportunities that will fall into your lap, and those you create for yourself. There are also the people you will need to help and assist throughout this amazing life. Yes, you. What do you think all those talents, gifts, and resources God gave you are for? They are meant for you to leave your mark in the world and in the lives of others. It's easy to lose sight of these things when you are overwhelmed and feeling consumed by your present circumstances. I can tell you first-hand that putting these wonderful aspects of your life on an indefinite, undefined hold, can and will have an adverse effect on you. It will look different for each of us. That constant nagging headache, backache, neck pain, swelling, and joint pain; that never-ending cold, weight gain, weight loss, feelings of sadness, feelings of resentment and bitterness, feeling inadequate, or full-blown depression. You get the point, and please know that the list of possible manifestations is endless, and the nature of the situation itself is non-discriminate.

In my own life, in my own FTL situation, I came to a crossroads. I knew God was doing a work in me through a series of circumstances, people, and events, and I had no idea I'd be sharing the outcome with you. I had no idea that what obstacles I could move beyond – and how I did so – would undoubtedly benefit countless others. Let's say millions of others. While FTL is a common term today, it's still fairly new as it relates to the trend, and while the number of young adults in this situation continue to rise, it's important to note that the number of people who kill their dreams, ignore their goals, and choose not to live a fulfilled life is nothing new at all. If you don't take on a posture of resilience and victory today, you could be sad and unsatisfied for a very long time; not to mention how sad and unsatisfied those around you will be as well.

Eight years ago, I sat at a table of ten at a local charity's fundraising event. The objective was to raise funds for child abuse prevention. I love charity events not only because of the cause and what it can mean in the lives of others, but also for the opportunity to meet new people. I'm always hopeful that there will be at least four people at my table whom I don't know.

When my husband and I sat down at the table initially, all the other guests were already seated. One particular woman never looked up as everyone at the table exchanged greetings and pleasantries. Her husband did, though. He looked up briefly, and I caught his sad but willing eyes. The event began, and the host gave announcements. I could only focus on the woman who still had her head down while the event host was talking.

As soon as the guests were released to get food, dance, and partake in the selection of activities created for the night, I took the vacated seat next to this woman. The first twenty minutes consisted of me doing most of the talking about my work in corporate America and my work now with young people and families. It wasn't until I heard myself sharing something personal about my family, which by the way was all God, that she looked up at me.

With a great deal of apprehension, she shared what was currently going on in her life. Her son had been making poor choices since high school, and then at the age of 32 was still living at home and making the same kinds of choices. The situation had sucked the life out of her and her relationship with her husband. Apparently, her husband was the one who insisted they attend the event that evening. The situation at home had also drained their finances. Her son doesn't work and spends most of all his day in front of the television. When he did venture out the house, he often found himself in trouble with the law.

She and her husband were an older couple. Their dreams of moving into a smaller home and doing some traveling weren't things they discussed anymore. They hadn't talked about anything with passion in years. She shared how she no longer went out with friends; that friends no longer invited her to go out with them. She did everything she could for her son with the hope that he would get it together. She prayed and had hoped for many years that God would help her son, but nothing had changed. She preferred not to talk with anyone, because conversations inevitably turned into conversations about family, kids, and grandkids at some point. Her son was her only child, and she was feeling hopeless and depressed.

By the end of our time together, her eyes were filled with tears. So were mine. We kept our emotions under wraps enough to not draw attention. When it became clear that the evening's festivities had come to an end, and our husbands were standing at the back of our chairs, respectively, we said our gentle goodbyes. The sadness and shame this sweet woman wore like an old comfy sweater is something I will never forget. We did not exchange contact information that night. I never felt led to ask, and neither did she. That moment was meant for her in whatever way God intended. That moment was also meant for me in the way God has been using it in my life since then. Working with young adults and their wonderful parents; meeting them where they are and assisting them in moving beyond their present circumstances.

No one is without challenges. It's unfortunate that folks are seemingly apathetic and judgmental until they find themselves in a similar circumstance. This always seems to be the case. One day you are judging a situation. You judge the people in the situation and how the people are handling the situation. You don't even have all the facts. Then one day, you find yourself in a place you never imagined you'd be. You want sympathy and compassion for what you are going through. You want folks to be kind in word and in deed, but then there's the ping in your heart when you realize that you weren't about any of that for others when you had the chance.

Now consider pausing to focus on what you're feeling right at this moment. If you feel a little conviction, great. Take stock in knowing that it's just that – gentle conviction, not condemnation. Know that yes, there is hope and that with the right tools and strategies, positive change is achievable and sustainable. The scripture Matthew 19:26 tells us that with God all things are possible. This time is not for you to feel bad about past choices, behaviors, or responses. It's certainly not about you continuing to swim in a river of shame and guilt. This is about focusing on all that's available to you, and what's possible for you and the ones you love.

In my obedience, I have embarked upon a journey to share and express love for you and yours through this book. Have you ever heard folks say that your tests become your testimony? It's a pretty common saying here in the Bible Belt and that's what writing this book is all about. Sharing with you so that you can benefit from my tests and glean from the lessons I've learned along the way. It's in the spirit of transparency that you will read about the many battles, and how addressing and overcoming some pretty important dynamics led to small wins along the way, and ultimately to the big victory that is mine today. If you are ready to do whatever you need to do to lay a new foundation that will assist and support you in a way that will also benefit your children, your significant other, and the many others in your life, this book is for you.

I pray that the stories and lessons in this book will enlighten and encourage you, guide and prepare you, and equally important, create a ripple that extends well beyond you that touches all you encounter.

Chapter 2:

Conditioned

———●——●———

"One day you will wake up and there won't be any more time to do the things you've always wanted. Do it now."
Paulo Coelho

So here you are, book in hand, hoping that I'll say something, anything, that will give you even the slightest hint into how you can better your current situation. Yes. Your adult child is home. In your home. The home you've given them. The home you've always told them is their safe place; where they can make all the mistakes they need to before they get out in the real world; where the consequences are great and sometimes overwhelming.

You know exactly what he or she is doing... what they seem to always do. You know it. You can close your eyes, and like through an antique reel-to-reel, you see the same scene that's been burned onto the backs of your lids from being played so many times. Your son or daughter is doing exactly what they want to do. That's usually not the productive thing. You know, the thing that could certainly help them make progress. It's typically the same dynamic. The things that are necessary for our adult child's life to begin to change, even improve slightly, don't get done and the excuse is always the same.

Believe me, I know what it's like to have your eyes transfixed to the pages in front of you. Your eyes soaking up every word while you hold your breath with anticipation for the aha statement or message that will catapult you and everything you love and desire into a dimension of bliss. Yeah sure, all while your adult child is home and being held captive by something or feeling completely paralyzed by only God knows what.

Depending on where you are in your life walk and spiritual journey, you may or may not know that we are not designed to nor are we created to carry worry. Nope. We are not. I can tell you, as someone who has an intimate relationship with God, that he made provisions early on through his son Jesus Christ, for us to give our cares and concerns over to him. This way we can remain open and at peace to live a life free from the burdens and strongholds that can undoubtedly keep us from living an abundant and prosperous life. Ha! Yeah, right! That's all we have to do? Hand over our cares to Jesus. Easy, right? No indeed. Not for most of us, anyway. But really, if we know this, why do we constantly do it? Why do we carry and shoulder the burden of life, shame, guilt, responsibility, and whatever else keeps us from sleeping, maintaining focus, taking good care of ourselves, and just simply making the kinds of decisions that can undoubtedly change, and even propel our lives to a better, more fulfilling one? I don't know what your answer is, but mine is simple and I'm happy to share it.

For the past 14 years, I have successfully suppressed every bit of thought, energy, and desire intended to manifest the destiny and greatness God created within me. We – and, yes this includes you too – cannot possibly live a truly fulfilled life when we do not respond and act upon that thing God called us to do. It's that thing that does not feel comfortable. It's that thing that will require you to step outside of your comfort zone, and even expose yourself in a very vulnerable way. So what do we do? We ignore it. Not right away. At first, we entertain it in our minds and even get excited about it. With that same 'ole antique reel-to-reel we play that thing in our minds until... wait for it... it becomes scary and we become paralyzed. Doing that thing means something's got to change. Something's got to change in a big, overwhelming, seemingly impossible way.

I am instantly reminded of a day some years ago when my oldest daughter was back at home after having thoroughly enjoyed twenty-thousand dollars' worth of college. I hope you know what I mean by thoroughly enjoyed. She had been acting out and being defiant. She was disrespectful at times and sometimes carried the air of a young person entitled to more than she had earned or deserved for that matter. It had been a tough day filled with flippant remarks, rising tensions and a clear power struggle. I mean, there was no way you could live in a house with old-school parents and talk to us any kind of way, and behave like you were the one who was in charge. This is how we old-school parents did it. Right? Well, I thought so.

That evening, well after midnight, my daughter thought it was acceptable to leave the house and go out. When I politely rejected the idea, the ugly words began. After about three rounds of back and forth – two rounds too many – my daughter solicited the support of her father and guess what...

you got it. He let her go out. Yes, this violates every rule of parenting, but the real question is this: What am I going to do in this situation? Clearly something had to change in a big, overwhelming, and seemingly impossible way.

Now get this. I asked this same daughter to do a cleaning task in the house. You should know that she was not working at the time and enjoyed a great deal of television throughout the day. She didn't respond to my request, and instead called her dad to complain that I asked her to do things I didn't ask either of my other two children to do. Here's the challenge. It's not that she made the call, but that my husband called me to voice my daughter's complaint.

OK, OK, OK. I need to make this clear. These stories are not about my husband, nor my daughter. They are about me. It's about how I've conditioned my loved ones, and how I respond to the situations and circumstances I am faced with. You can make judgment all you want, but I'm looking at the man in the mirror. Something clearly had to change in a big, overwhelming, and seemingly impossible way.

I'm a Stephen Covey gal. I was one of the first to attend his leadership training back when The 7 Habits of Highly Effective People was first released in 1989. The Habits that come to mind in my situation fall under Independence, which include the first three habits: Be Proactive, Begin with the End in Mind, and Put First Things First. Well, that said, I want you to know what I proactively put first, with the end in mind. And that, my friend, is what I call conditioning. Yes, to condition in its true Webster definition: "To have a significant influence on or determine the manner or outcome of something." I know full well that I've conditioned my children to listen or not listen to the things I say. I've conditioned them – and my husband for that matter – to know exactly what responses and behaviors to expect from me. See. That's it right there.

We decide how to condition our bodies. We simply change our diet and begin an exercise regimen. We decide how to condition our ability to hear from God more clearly by spending more time praying, worshiping and studying God's word. We condition our ability to increase our effectiveness and productivity by adopting new, powerful habits like waking up early to exercise and plan out our day. It takes effort but conditioning is something that can be applied to every area of our lives. Want better relationships? Condition yourself by intentionally spending more time with those you care to have a richer relationship with.

So, back to how conditioning was a key component to how I needed to address the situation at 190 Bridgestone Cove. Breaking the Habit of Being Yourself by Dr. Joe Dispenza, is one of my favorite books and was introduced to me by a relationship counselor I admire a great deal. This book is highly effective in changing your mindset around the behaviors you've conditioned yourself to for pretty much most of your life. Ideally, if you can pause and intentionally do things you don't normally do, at a time when you would normally be doing something else, that's a great beginning to shaking things up.

My family had become conditioned, like anyone I interact or engage with, to how I behave and respond in most situations. Even the people I serve with know how I will respond to people in need. The people I work with know before they ask how I will respond to a request or work dynamic. That includes my church family and my girlfriends from back in the day. I've not only conditioned myself to be who I am through my responses and behaviors, I've conditioned those around me to expect the very same. The time was overdue for something to change in a big, overwhelming, seemingly impossible way…and that something was me.

It's not so easy to look at ourselves. I'm at a point where I absolutely love it. It wasn't always this way, but I tell you, it feels so good to watch how things change instantly when I intentionally do something no one expects me to do. It could be as simple as responding to a request in a different way, or simply choosing to remain silent when I would normally be highly vocal. Even more impactful is when I veer from my normal routine. I've even had people apologize for getting ahead of a situation because they were pretty certain about what I was going to do in a particular situation. When I did something very different from what they expected of me, they were surprised. While the essence of who I am in Christ remains the same, I am living my life, my truth, and not the one others expect me to live.

Back to being a Stephen Covey gal. Most of you know that Mr. Covey came out with an 8th habit, From Effectiveness to Greatness. Here's an overview statement relative to finding your voice:

> *"The essence of this habit is that you will find your voice when you can say you are 100% involved with what you are doing in your life, so that your body, mind, heart and spirit are all engaged in whatever is important to you. To find your voice, you need to examine your natural talent, what you absolutely love to do, what really interests you.*

And you must listen to the confirming inner voice of your
conscience that tells you what is the right thing to do."

I love this! I believe that if you are 100% involved, then you can shift gears at any time. You can always consider and do what you absolutely love and not what you've always done or what others have come to expect you to do. That pertains to everything, especially your voice, or absence thereof. What if you chose not to respond when you would typically have much to say?

In Proverbs 10:19, the Bible says that when there are lots of words, sin is unavoidable. What if you chose to respond in love instead of judgement? Ooooo, that's a big one. Please consider that there is a root cause to why people behave and respond the way they do. We'll talk more about that in a later chapter, but in the meantime, the bottom line is that every person, especially those we love and respect, are amazing expressions of God's love – even though we may not like them or the things they do, very much at times.

The relationship with my oldest daughter had been a challenge for some years. I love my first-born dearly. I admire her strength and her beauty, inside and out. I hope with all my heart that she knows this, although it doesn't always seem like it. She has expended quite a bit of energy to be the exact opposite of me. Family would say things like "she'll find her way" or "mothers and daughters are like that in the beginning sometimes, and then it changes when the daughter gets older." OK, how old is older? The years were rolling by, and I spent way too much time reminding her of that. Why did I keep doing that when I knew that each time it would be met with resentment and harsh words? Because

I was hopeful, not hopeless. I also got the wool pulled over my eyes more times than I care to share. I couldn't help but believe her when she'd give a detailed description of her plans to turn things around. She'd even tell me, very convincingly mind you, when these plans were going to unfold, and like the hopeful mom, I'd believe her.

I want to challenge you to begin a process of conditioning yourself, to break the habit of being you. Please don't misunderstand: I am not suggesting that you are the problem, or that even your adult child or your spouse is the problem. I am not pointing any fingers at anyone, nor would I encourage you to do that. I'm just laying a foundation for change and ultimately a peace that leads to greatness in every area of your life.

Chapter 3:

New Lenses

———●——●———

"If you don't like something, change it. If you can't change it, change your attitude."
MAYA ANGELOU

As this book unfolds, we will look at our values and perceptions while taking inventory of our inherent and external resources to begin to move from concept to action. It's one thing to know the changes we'd like to see in our lives, and it's another to know and understand how to accomplish them. Even after we know and understand how, we have to do something for things to happen and ultimately change. Motivation is a concept. You need to feel motivated to do something but you don't just decide you are motivated and then miraculously you start moving into action. No. It takes more than that for most of us.

It's amazing how different life and people can look to you in the wake of a significant life event. How things that once seemed to matter and occupy a fair amount of your thought life, no longer have a place, and in some cases become completely forgotten. Your relationships and outlook on life are forever changed, and you consider whether you are spending your time in the way that God intended for you to.

Is what you are doing meaningful and making a difference in the lives of others?

The loss of my sister was the significant life event for me; it actually began the day we received the diagnosis that she had ALS, an ugly, brutal and unforgiving disease. Unexpectedly, the mourning began quite early, during the caregiving phase. It was clear I had lost my best friend, so far in advance of us laying her to rest. Life doesn't go on hold while you are trying to keep a loved one comfortable, and helping to maintain some semblance of control and independence in their life. Life doesn't go on hold while you're grieving. I am happy that my sister is disease-free and no longer in pain. But her absence is still overwhelming.

My sister was my oldest daughter's Godmother, as well as her auntie. She supported my daughter in everything, and was a wonderful cheerleader and confidant for her as well. She attended every concert, every sporting event, and every milestone. You name it and my sister, Monique, was there.

As my daughter got older, it was wonderful to see her use my sister as a shoulder and sounding board. It's great when your child has someone you love and trust to talk with. It's healthy when there is another adult that shares your value system and easily and lovingly imparts them into your child. My daughter got to a point where she shared more with my sister than with me. That was fine; especially since I was always made aware of anything I needed to address or be concerned about. You realize how much you took for granted when someone you love is gone. I wonder if my daughter feels the same now that her aunt Moe Moe is no longer with us.

This reminds me of these words: "The collapse of character begins with compromise." Being true to who we are is critical to our success in this journey. You know you better than anyone else. You and I will need to agree right now that we won't compromise in any aspect of what we're expected to do. We won't compromise our integrity by way of short cuts nor will we compromise by way of negative thinking. Know that the work required in each chapter can prove to be challenging and uncomfortable at times, but it is very necessary to making the changes you've been dreaming about for way too long. I wasn't willing to compromise my truth, my relationships, my success, nor my destiny. I was not willing to play small and neither should you.

We are going to gain clarity on what drives and feeds our current circumstances. We're going to gain clarity on what drives and motivates us. We're going to gain clarity on what drives and motivates anyone else who plays a significant role in the circumstances and situations we are currently dealing with.

Imagine that. Have you ever noticed how much more effective you are in managing or dealing with a situation when you fully understand everything and everyone involved? It relates back to Stephen Covey's 5th Habit: Seek first to understand, then be understood. You'll understand how critical this is to our process as we move along.

The prescription for your new lenses may not have come after one specific or significant life event. It could have evolved over time simply from you being immersed in or exposed to one situation or dynamic for an extended period of time. It's like the experience of working for years under a manager or supervisor who lacks interpersonal skills and who is unprofessional and disrespectful at work. Perhaps it's experiencing years of being in a loveless marriage. One could even look at living from paycheck to paycheck for most of your adult life as an example.

These are negative examples, I know. That's what I'm choosing to focus on for our new lenses. You see, for most of us, when you experience a significant life event, or some challenging circumstance for an extended period of time, you will most likely get to a point of no return. That place that has a sign on the front gate that says enough is enough! That place where you feel completely exhausted by what is, and you are hoping and looking forward to what will be. When we get there, when we know something has to be done differently so we can experience a different outcome, we find ourselves ready, open and coachable. By the way, the point of no return has a cliff that folks tend to gravitate to, not when they feel hopeless, but when they feel hopeful. They are ready to take the leap. If you're feeling like the time is right for you, take the leap. I'll catch you! It may take reading through a few more chapters or even getting to the end of this book, but you'll be fine. Better than fine.

The objective is to increase everything that is good. With our new lenses, we'll be able to identify those things which are good and bring them into abundance. Another one of my favorite quotes is from Gautama Buddha: "If you knew what I know about the power of giving, you would not let a single meal pass without sharing it in some way." Don't you love that? There's an opportunity here. I give to you, and then you give to others. It will undoubtedly come back to me, and you, in a good way. It's a wonderful never-ending cycle of love expressed through sharing, giving and fellowship. It helps to give meaning to our life.

Most importantly, I believe it provides the key ingredient to the foundation of our successes. Love. That's where everything stems from. You love something, someone, some dynamic, some cause, some circumstance, and then there you go... doing something in a way that promotes everything good about that thing or that person. We have to first increase our own good. Our good thoughts need to overshadow the negative ones. We can condition ourselves to respond in good, positive ways and not self-defeating ways. You've heard the saying that "attitude is everything." Right? It's important to have a good handle on your attitude. It governs the way you perceive the world and the way the world perceives you. Charles Swindoll, author of The Grace Awakening said, "We cannot change the inevitable. The only thing we can do is play on the one string we have, and that is our attitude. I am convinced that life is 10% what happens to me and 90% of how I react to it. And so it is with you...we are in charge of our attitudes." It wouldn't fare me or my husband well if we responded to each other in negative, self-defeating ways during times of stress and frustration. I use to always tell my staff, when they were dealing with difficult clients, "behavior dictates behavior." Oftentimes, what you give is what you get.

With all this talk of positive action and behavior, I can't help but think of Rotary International. I am a Fellow Rotarian, and I have a high degree of respect for our four-way test. If you don't know what a Rotarian is, it's an active member of a worldwide charitable society of business and professional people. The Rotary four-way test states: Of the things we think, say or do (1) is it the truth? (2) is it fair to all concerned? (3) will it build goodwill and better friendships? (4) will it be beneficial to all concerned? I think this would be a beneficial motto for everyone to consider in their daily life walk. My club members and I recite it together at the end of every weekly meeting. I find myself considering it often and especially when I have to make tough decisions. You may find it useful as well.

Many folks offered their love, prayers, and condolences when my sister passed away. Some shared how they couldn't begin to imagine my pain, especially since they have a sister whom they love dearly. They continue with saying that they couldn't imagine their life without her. That's something isn't it? If you consider what is going on right now in your life; your adult child is still at home when you think he or she should be out and on their own; maybe you don't feel supported by your significant other and the two of you often don't always see eye to eye. OK, but could you imagine your life without them? Man, the things we take for granted. Things can change in a minute and if we would only consider changing our perception now, things could change drastically for the better, even now too.

Have you given any thought at all to what it would cost you to not be here and move in this direction? Have you considered how much time has gone by already with you and those you care about being in a constant state of flux and dissension? I hope the answers to these questions have created a reality check that fuels your efforts and keeps you motivated and energized during this process. So much of what you can achieve depends on it. Pay attention and take notes in the tools at the end of each chapter that relate to the steps in the process. You'll be gathering tools and increasing your repertoire.

So, get ready. There is also a little Personal Prescription at the end of each step. We're going to dig deep and stand tall. Dig deep into the open and painful spots of our current situation, and stand tall and confident through it all – even when we don't feel like it. We're going to cover the basis of 7 steps that allowed me to successfully overcome the challenges I was experiencing at home and at work. The order in which we address each step is intentional. You're going to need some quiet time, a quiet place, and a quiet spirit; one that is ready to receive. Quite frankly, there's too much at stake to not be.

Steps

Chapter 4:

Marinating in Thought

●●

*"I will not let anyone walk through my mind
with their dirty feet."*
MAHATMA GANDHI

You know how people say that words don't matter?
That's a crock, because they absolutely do. Words seep
deeply into our souls and into our mental vault where
we can access them whenever we need to feel better about or
sorry for ourselves. I mean, we do love to get pumped up as
much as we love pity parties. Don't we?

You may not be aware of this but there's not one place
in the Bible, nope, not one place at all, where Jesus speaks
negatively about himself. And despite what others said about
him, good, bad, or otherwise, he never wavered on who he
was or, for that matter, the purpose of his existence. Why do
I use Jesus as an example? Well, if we are to operate in his
likeness where love, joy, peace, patience, kindness, goodness,
faithfulness, gentleness, and self-control are the fruit we
produce in our daily lives, then we have absolutely got to be
kinder in our dealings with ourselves.

If you and I are anything alike, there's a tendency
to believe that certain things have to be in place, certain

circumstances have to exist, or that certain people have to do a certain thing, or be a certain way even, before we can feel empowered or motivated to take action and move... in any direction. Life is not a game of dominos. Most things don't have prerequisites; especially when it comes to you taking the steps you know will be game-changers at home, at work, and in your community. Yeah, yeah, I know we're more likely to be successful when we are best prepared for whatever it is we've committed ourselves to do or have to deal with or experience. But if that thing we talked about in the previous chapter is going to happen anyway – if that thing needs to be responded to anyway – then having the confidence to move beyond scary and paralyzed to boldly and confidently facing that thing head on, is paramount to real and lasting change.

There was a chapter in my life when I would repeatedly find myself in the hospital due to an allergic reaction of some sort. My tongue would swell to a size larger than my mouth could accommodate. My face became something unrecognizable. Things had gotten pretty concerning. I would wake at two or three in the morning, drooling and trying to manage the oversized tongue in my mouth.

There was always a mad rush to the hospital because the tingle in my throat was an indicator that my throat was beginning to close. Once the ambulance would arrive at my home, the paramedics would immediately begin to give me injections of epinephrine. I'd arrive at the hospital feeling high as a kite and falling asleep shortly thereafter. I'd wake to find my sister by my side. I recall that she was always mad at me. She later explained that she didn't want me to die. This is the same sister that passed away due to ALS.

Anyway, my sister was always by my side and wanted to know how we were going to go about finding the cause of this craziness I would experience at least 3 times or more a year. Well, I visited many doctors, all specialists in their field. I gave what felt like gallons of blood only to discover I had something called Raynaud's Syndrome and anticardiolipin antibodies. However, no one could explain the terrible, life-threatening swelling that would happen to me in the early morning hours and at other odd times during the day. I remember volunteering in the media center in the middle school one of my children attended, and at the check-out counter a student asked me what was happening to my face. I could feel the familiar tingling and knew something was about to go down, but I thought that if I ignored it, the episode wouldn't gain momentum. I ended up in the hospital that afternoon.

This went on for about a year when a nurse friend of mine recommended I see a medical specialist in Atlanta. I had seen my fair share of doctors and had given more than my fair share of blood, so, no, I wasn't enthused about seeing this person. I knew my friend was concerned and had cashed in some high-stake chips to make the arrangement, so I went. This doctor didn't ask for my medical records. He didn't order any tests, or have his nurse take any blood. He simply introduced himself, listened patiently to my explanation of what had been happening to me over the course of the year, and then asked me, "What are you thinking about right before you fall asleep?" That question was life changing for me. Truly life changing. He went on to explain how if we are not careful, we can actually marinate in the thoughts we go to sleep with, whether good or bad. I want you to know that since that day, I go to bed every night reading and meditating on the word of God. That's right. I read or listen to scripture every night before I fall asleep. Let me give you the crux of my testimony. Ready? I haven't had another episode since.

So, I came to a place in my life where I decided to go back to that thing God called me to do as early back as my teenage years. That place was a crossroads called life and death, and the reality of how much time I had allowed to pass, not wasted mind you, hit me like a hail ball in Georgia, and caused me to feel a twinge of concern for what my future would look like. Crossroads are a tricky intersection of roads. On the one hand, you get to choose which road to take. You are, however, aware that you can actually get to your destination by taking any of the roads before you, and so the choice is really all about how long you actually want your journey to be.

Now I'm not saying I wasn't productive or didn't experience success in the years leading up to writing this book. Shoot, no! I served honorably in the United States Air Force; married my high school sweetheart; bought a big ole' house; and gave birth to three beautiful children, all while climbing the proverbial corporate ladder. No. What I'm saying is that I didn't do what I was called to do. I didn't honor and fully acknowledge what God had created me to be. And here's the thing. It doesn't matter how long you ignore and move around that thing. God will always bring it back around and remind you of it. What that reminder looks like has everything to do with how you best learn life's lessons. I have to say that my lessons are sometimes painful.

How many times have you reached your destination only to realize three things: First, that you have no idea how you got there. You can't recall the turns, the hills and valleys, or even some of the people along the way. Secondly, you know the journey to your destination could have been considerably shorter. You begin to think of the countless opportunities and choices you could have made, and ultimately feel a tremendous sense of regret about them. Thirdly, you realize that where you've arrived is no longer where you want to be. It's right there, at that very moment, that how you respond to this realization, will make all the difference in how you recover and experience everything going forward, in the best possible way.

We sometimes find ourselves in the weeds of our everyday life, right? We find ourselves way too focused on what other people are doing and saying, instead of maintaining the big picture view of our goals and dreams. We get easily frustrated and feel stuck when people don't go along with our plans, and we sometimes get easily distracted and are undisciplined in our habits and behaviors. OK, so you can't relate? Sure. Well, if you sincerely want a life where you actually feel the freedom you already have; actually ignite the power resources you already have, and actually move toward your dreams being manifested in your life, then you've opened the right book. I'm happy that our paths have crossed and I do not believe that it's by chance. I believe that we are going to do great things... that thing together.

So what are you thinking about consistently? If you are solely focused on the negative aspects of your adult children being at home, then most likely they will be there longer than you care for them to be. That's just how the universe works. It draws to you what you focus on most. If you are constantly thinking about how you would like your life partner to be more supportive, which implies that he or she is not, then most definitely you will receive more of what you don't want. Consider this for a moment. When you are feeling your best and thinking your best thoughts on any given day, what kind of day do you ultimately have? I would bet money that it's a pretty good day. Isn't it true that when your attitude isn't in the right place and you are focused on all that is seemingly wrong and what could go wrong, that it ultimately will go wrong? Henry Ford said, "Whether you think you can or whether you think you can't, you're right." Scholars expound on his quote: Self-confidence is a powerful thing. When Henry Ford made this quote, he was saying just this. He was literally making a bold statement to let others around him know that one of the primary keys to getting what you want out of life is believing that you can have it.

As human beings, we are wired to follow in what we think and what we believe. If we believe in and think on the positive about ourselves, our actions will surely follow this route in life. On the other hand, thinking that we cannot do or achieve something also sets us on a course to fail and fall short. Despite what some may try to argue, a person's own mind is one of the strongest influences that will ever be present in their life.

If I want any aspect of what goes on at 190 Bridgestone Cove to be different, I think about and meditate on what that different, happy, successful place looks like. Seem hokey to you? Well, that's unfortunate because it absolutely works, and it can work for you too. It's not magic, it's just an understanding that what we think and focus on is actually what we can manifest and draw into our lives. It is one hundred percent true. Like I said, it's not magic. Some things take longer than others and so much of it depends on how you think about it, how you feel about it, and what you marinate in. Like I said in the first chapter, I'm not talking about young adults with the challenges associated with anxiety and other mental illnesses. I'm also not talking about the ones who are doing well for themselves and are choosing to live at home for a host of reasons, and with the blessing of their parents. I'm talking about the ones who are lazy, unwilling, or perhaps not yet mature. The ones who are just simply not ready! Connect with me sometime and I'll show you a photo of me at my worst before meditating on the wonderful, life-affirming word of God.

I'd like to suggest that you take this to bed with you. Consider that what you are thinking about before you go to bed, you are allowing your mind to marinate in it while you sleep. That's a pretty big deal to me. Do you really want your mind marinating in the energy and thoughts of the miserable person you have to deal with at work? Do you really want your mind to marinate on the situation you are dealing with at home with your adult children? If you do marinate on your adult children, how about focusing your thoughts toward them in a positive way with images of them working, living on their own, and sustaining themselves? Sounds good to me. Let's go with that thought!

Personal Prescription

There are studies that prove that our brain is more inclined to "get stuck" on a negative thought than it would on a positive one. The negative thought can actually become programmed into our subconscious and ultimately replayed in our minds for decades. It can be challenging to replace a negative thought or negative memory with a positive one, but with practice, over and over again, day after day, it certainly can be done. If we can couple the new, positive thought with an equally positive feeling or emotion, we've got an unstoppable combination. At the end of what you perceive as a long and stressful day, resist the urge to recount all the bad, negative things that happened that day. Instead, ask yourself, "what happened today that was good?" Actually answer the question. You may be surprised to find that your day was pretty decent after all. By doing this, we can begin to avoid creating new, negative thoughts that can easily make their way to being stuck in our subconscious mind.

Chapter 5:

Barriers Have Names

———— ● ● ————

"Our prime purpose in this life is to help others.
And if you can't help them, at least don't hurt them."

DALAI LAMA

My breathing sped up as I watched the garage door move. It opened slowly, body part by body part, revealing a pair of shoes, legs, and ultimately the torso and head of one of my neighbors. The moment I heard a car door slam in the driveway on the other side of the garage door, I knew that someone – more than likely this particular neighbor – would be standing on the other side.

It was obvious that she could hardly wait to vomit some new information all over me. So there we are, with no garage door between us, in what could be construed as a western style stand-off. She waited a moment before speaking. When she finally spoke, her words were sharp and crisp. Her daughter, who graduated with mine, had been accepted by her first-choice college.

My neighbor wasn't excited to tell me because she thought I would be happy for her, or because she was a humble, yet proud mother looking to share her good news and joy with a friend. No indeed. She and I were not friends.

We were neighbors. There's a difference, you know. She was looking to make me feel jealous, bad, sad, or all three. She knew the challenges my husband and I were having with our oldest child and for her, that was even more reason to share her good news. I could tell she was basking in the moment; watching my face for the slightest hint of sadness or envy. Our eyes stayed locked, and when I blinked, I congratulated her and wished the best for her, her daughter, and her family. I heard myself speak a few more words. Funny, at the moment I can't quite remember what they were. I do recall that at the same time I was speaking those final words, I had opened my car door and was climbing inside. You see, I knew this neighbor wasn't going to ask me about my daughter. She believed whatever her daughter shared with her about mine, and she wasn't the least bit interested in being a friendly, honest, resource.

That exchange with my neighbor, was like so many others, where the outcome was always the same. Me feeling ashamed or inadequate in some way. Folks would never really know how I was feeling, because I had become a master at putting on the happy face.

That day was a turning point for me. Constant feelings of shame, inadequacy, and let's add, guilt to the mix while we're at it, had become exhausting. Absolutely exhausting. Comparing my family, my children, my spouse, myself, my anything and everything, to anyone else, served no one well; especially me. The comparison game is deceitful. You totally forget that you are a unique expression of God's love, and that you came into this world at an appointed time for an appointed purpose. That you are equipped with gifts and talents beautifully packaged with a spirit of power, and of love, and of a sound mind. This is from scripture 2 Timothy 1:7. Yes indeed, that exchange was a turning point for me.

What if my daughter was like other young ladies her age? What if she made the kinds of choices other students who seem to have a good head on their shoulders made? What if the harsh words and actions of others glided right over our heads as smoothly as a figure skater over ice? What if the opinions of others didn't weigh so heavily in our minds? What if we didn't need someone else's approval or need to feel validated by them? What if we only concerned ourselves with what God thinks?

The things, the people, and the circumstances we find ourselves beholden to are really barriers to our ability to transcend the way we live and love. It is necessary to give these barriers names and call them out. We need to call them what they are and move beyond them. We need to speak our truth about these barriers so they can no longer have power over us. Until we do, they will continue to, ever so seductively, keep us where we're at. In your life you know exactly what their names are; exactly what to call them. The names are circling around in your head as you read these words. Don't limit the names to just people. The barriers can be things, like the ones you may find yourself addicted to. The barriers can also be places and situations you feel drawn to but again, no longer serve you well.

I imagine it would be pretty easy to just identify and give names to our barriers, and then do nothing with the information. That would certainly be the road of least resistance, not the road of transformation and victory you're working towards, but I get it. We're tired and overwhelmed by our circumstances, and now we're stretched mentally and emotionally. When I gave my barriers names it was a true aha moment for me. I only became exhausted when I knew I had to do something about them, and so I traveled the road to victory anyway.

As barriers are roadblocks of sorts, keeping us from our destinations, our destiny if you will, boundaries, on the other hand, are the healthy cousins. Boundaries establish a framework for healthy living so you can set an expectation for how you want to be treated. They are a necessary component in all healthy relationships. Often times in our attempts to set boundaries, we create barriers. Dr. Brene Brown, a research professor at the University of Houston says, "daring to set boundaries is about the courage to love ourselves even when we risk disappointing others." Being able to clearly define and establish for others what is acceptable and what is not acceptable when it comes to interacting with you, and engaging with you in any way, is integral to our success in this process.

Equally important is never compromising on where those boundaries lie because the moment you compromise, that's the very moment you send a different message to the universe and to others. People can and will take advantage when boundaries are not established. People will also take advantage if you're always oscillating like a fan. On some days your boundaries matter to you and you defend them like your life depends on it, and other days, not so much. Consistency is the key here. Going forward, let's switch the fan from oscillate mode to steady.

We know how hard it is to make difficult decisions and that dealing with triggers can be even harder. Triggers seem to come out of nowhere and take on so many different forms

– smells, words, pictures, people, music, events, you name it! Triggers not only blindside us, the reactions we have to them seem to do the same. Have you ever responded to a trigger in such a way that the people involved have absolutely no idea why you overacted? It seems they've forgotten the part they've played in who you are today and why you respond to things the way you do; more than likely they were never aware in the first place. At least that's what we think and all that does is add fuel to the fire. We are not, and do not have to be, defined by our past. Triggers can cause you to say things you can't take back and cause you to do things you're sure to regret. I have done both. What about you? Then after the experience is over and many hours have passed you can't help but wonder for yourself why you reacted in the over-the-top way that you did. How in the world do we prepare for something as sneaky as triggers? That takes prep work. It takes some serious prep work, and like me, you can do it.

It takes a high level of awareness to not let our past experiences and responses define our future responses. It takes us back to Chapter 2 where we talked about conditioning and the fact that we can choose our behaviors and that ultimately through our behaviors and responses we condition others to know exactly what to expect from us.

Once I decided to acknowledge, address, and begin the process of removing the barriers in my life, it became easier to do after each one. It also felt like a weight was being lifted from my neck and shoulders, and no longer was playing small or accepting the status quo an option.

Now, getting back to the neighbor. What she didn't know, and probably still doesn't, is that I absolutely love young people. I love it when they succeed, and I always celebrate their accomplishments. I feel honored when I have opportunities to pour into them and support their efforts. Her daughter is no exception. I am thrilled that she has a full ride to the college of her choice, and I feel confident that she'll succeed in whatever she puts her heart and mind to. It was my neighbor's behavior and ill intentions that had me feeling the way I felt that day, and would I love for my daughter to have the same wonderful experience as her daughter? You bet I would, but what I have learned is that we all (including our children) will have our own wonderful, unique life and learning experiences, and I wouldn't have it any other way. Any other mindset might suggest that I am ungrateful and unappreciative of the many blessings I have in my life. My cup runneth over, and it's vitally important to me that how I live my life is an expression of how thankful I am to God.

Personal Prescription

Healthy boundaries are an integral component to self-care in all aspects of our lives. Boundaries can be defined as the limits we set with other people, which indicate what we find acceptable and unacceptable in their behavior towards us. Knowing our boundaries generally comes from a healthy sense of self-worth in a way that is not contingent on other people or the feelings they have toward us. The consequences of not setting healthy boundaries can include stress, financial burdens, wasted time, and certainly relationship issues. So what do healthy boundaries look like? That answer depends on the setting. If we stay focused on the parent-young adult relationship, it might look like a parent asking their adult child to not take the parent's car without asking. As for the adult child, he or she might ask their parents to never enter the adult child's room without permission. Once you start naming barriers in your life, if it is not feasible or realistic to remove the barrier from your life, then setting and maintaining healthy boundaries is an absolute must.

Barriers Have Names Worksheet

Instructions: Fill in the table as follows - in the column on the left list the goals you'd like to achieve and the dreams you'd like to become a reality. In the column on the right fill in the why or the name of whatever or whomever is a barrier to achieving the goal or dream that corresponds in the column on the left. There's one example to help you get started. Take your time with this and definitely keep notes about what you are thinking and how you are feeling as you go through this exercise. I look forward to you and me coming back to it later.

Goal/Dream	Barrier - Who/What/Why
Starting my new business.	Me - get out of my way.

Goal/Dream	Barrier - Who/What/Why

Chapter 6:

Good & Plenty

———●●———

"The time is coming when each of us will have to give an account of our stewardship."
SUNDAY ADELAJA

Most people associate stewardship only with money and budgets. Being a good steward has more to do with everything you've been blessed with in the way of gifts, talents, resources, opportunities, leadership, relationships – pretty much everything. If you really want to experience the best of everything, every aspect of your life, you must consider stewardship.

When we prepared our oldest to go to college, her village surrounded her. It was a struggle, but she got her SAT scores to a place where she could continue her education at a Georgia University. We celebrated this milestone with her and she had everything any new college student could ask for. Her meal plan was in place. Her tuition was covered by Mr. & Mrs. yours truly. Her dorm room was to be decorated with sophistication. She had all the books and supplies she would need. She had a bank account for incidentals, unexpected expenses, and emergencies. She even had a new wardrobe. So we packed up the family van and all of us, siblings included, took my oldest daughter to college.

My daughter was well into her first semester when it was clear that we were going to have to go pick her up from school and bring her home. The need to have fun outweighed academics and studies tenfold. Her actions, behavior, choices – including the lies – made for painful circumstances. My husband and I are still paying for her choices. Back then she had not been a good steward of all that she has. It shouldn't be typical for anyone to take their family, their friends, their colleagues, their home, their job, their faith, or the opportunities they are afforded for granted. Yet I watch people, adults especially, do it every single day.

Stewardship is the careful and responsible management of something entrusted to one's care. This includes your relationships. Imagine how much deeper and richer your relationships would be if you spend the time necessary to cultivate and strengthen them; if you were always respectful, humble, and grateful in your dealings with others. Good stewardship includes the many opportunities you've been given, whether or not you recognize them as opportunities. There are things we are to be obedient and act upon, yet we choose disobedience or the lazy road.

Our jobs? Yes. Our jobs. With so many people looking for jobs today, why would anyone take theirs for granted? It comes with a paycheck that provides a resource for you; there are colleagues for you to inspire, encourage and learn from; there is a dynamic in the workplace that affords you an opportunity to add value in some way. Of course, I am aware that not everyone makes enough money at their jobs, and that some colleagues are miserable and hard, OK, super miserable and hard to get along with. I also know that not all jobs are stimulating. However, none of this changes the fact that it is a gift. An absolute blessing that we are called to treat with the utmost care and to be thankful for.

An essay by Bill Peel at The High Calling suggests there are four principals to biblical stewardship. The first is ownership. In the beginning, God creates everything and then puts Adam in charge of it all; to look after it, work it, and take care of it. There is an element of obedience in this. What God gives you and places under your control is meant for you to be a good steward of. The second is responsibility. In his essay Peel writes, "Although God gives us "all things richly to enjoy," nothing is ours. Nothing really belongs to us. God owns everything; we're responsible for how we treat it and what we do with it." We are called to be good stewards of what belongs to God. Third is the principal of accountability. We are entrusted with much and should not expect to manage and care only as we see fit. Exercising our stewardship should be under the watchful eye of our Creator. We are called to give an account for how we manage all we've been given, including our time, money, abilities, information, wisdom, relationships, and authority. Lastly, Peel acknowledges the principal of reward. In Colossians 3:23-24 Paul writes: "Whatever you do, work at it with all your heart, as working for the Lord, not for men, since you know that you will receive an inheritance from the Lord as a reward. It is the Lord Christ you are serving." We are shown time and time again how good and faithful stewards are rewarded. You see them by their fruit. The same fruit we talked about in Chapter 4.

Back when I worked as a Director for Deloitte, I was part of the Disaster Preparedness Team, and after both terrorist attacks on the World Trade Center, 1993 and 2001, respectively, the team was expected to account for the whereabouts and safety of all of our employees. You know the devastation that took place. The fear and anxiety that gripped me as I tried desperately to reach the 178 people who worked directly for me was indescribable. They were my team, my support group, my work family. They celebrated me in such a big way when I was pregnant with my first child, the daughter I've been referring to since you started reading this book. From the day they each began their individual career with the company, they were mine to be responsible for in the workplace; to help them navigate the corporate waters; to mentor; to advocate for and to defend when necessary. On September 11th, I knew where they were all expected to be and at what times on that horrific day. I know where I was supposed to be on that day – on the 94th floor of Two World Trade. We lost so much on that horrific day, and we will never forget. I've since left Deloitte, such a great company, and I am forever grateful for all I learned during my career there. One of those lessons being good stewardship.

My spouse has been entrusted to me as well. There used to be a time when I would like for things to be different. You know what I'm talking about. If only he or she would... you fill in the blank. If only he or she could be more like... you fill in the blank on that one too. How ridiculous was that! Well, it probably doesn't seem so ridiculous when you are immersed in a situation you'd rather not be in, especially if you feel quite sure that if he or she was more supportive, or if he or she did things differently, things would be much different. Better even.

The chapter in my life where I felt this way has passed and opened the door for such peace and freedom I can't tell you. How I operated in that space during that time, and didn't have some kind of a breakdown is a mystery to me. I stopped concerning myself with God's business. He made it very clear that He is most capable of everything. I purchased a coffee mug from a Joyce Meyer conference about twelve years ago. I love it and still use it to this day. It says, "Good morning, this is God. I will be handling all of your problems today. I will not need your help, so have a miraculous day." It's funny because I lived my entire life, up until recently, trying to assist Him. If I could just get this person or that person to change or just get everyone to understand that my way is the right way, the best way, then all will be right in my world. Absolutely ridiculous and unreasonable, and it certainly never worked. My husband is awesome in all his spouse-ness. He does the best he can with what he knows and what he has. There is absolutely nothing more I can ask or hope for. He makes mistakes like the rest of us, and deserves forgiveness like the rest of us, too. I have expectations of him; he has expectations of me. While I would like him to remember my love language on his own, I no longer mind having to remind him every now and again.

At the beginning of a leadership conference I attended in the early 90s, well before having kids, I was asked to say my name and share what I believed was the primary reason for my success in such a busy and demanding role. My answer was simple: My husband. I shared that he supports me in everything I do, and that because of him, I have the flexibility to do what's needed to do my job with excellence. That was a long time ago, but it still holds true today. That doesn't mean that hubby and I haven't stumbled along the way. It's just my reality, and an example I love and hold onto.

Sharing is a huge aspect of stewardship. Being able to give of yourself, your time, your talents, and your resources, without expecting anything in return, is a beautiful thing. If you don't think so, try it. I bet you'll find that you end up getting more out of selflessly serving than those you are providing the service for.

There is a local nonprofit in my county that provides healthcare to the underserved and uninsured. They are a significant part of the safety net where I live. The people who run this organization are wonderful, loving people, and the volunteers who give their talents and time to share their expertise with thousands of people each year are nothing short of amazing. They are doctors from different specialties who give regular hours each month to see patients at no charge. Their deeds are generous. They positively impact the lives of those who cannot adequately help themselves, all while setting an amazing example for others to be inspired by and follow. Simone De Beauvoir said, "That's what I consider true generosity. You give your all, and yet you always feel as if it costs you nothing." The doctors who volunteer for this charitable organization have brought many other doctors into the fold, all because of the joy they have in serving and sharing. It's contagious and creates a ripple that can spread farther than any of them will ever know.

I don't know about you but at the end of the day, at the end of our days, I want to hear the Lord say to me, "Well done, good and faithful servant! You have been faithful with a few things; I will put you in charge of many things. Come and share your master's happiness!"

Personal Prescription

There was a two-year chapter in my life when I found myself taking inventory of the really hard things going on in my life. This chapter included the loss of my sister. I remember the very day when I heard myself vocalizing the list of hard things going on in my life during that time. I could hear myself in a way that had to be displeasing to God, as if I had absolutely nothing to be thankful for in the midst of trials. That was an absolute lie! I felt some conviction at the thought of how many times and with how many people I shared that terrible list. I had and still have blessings beyond measure. After hearing the displeasing sound of my own words, I committed that whenever lists were in order, I would vocalize my list of blessings only. It's a pretty powerful thing, that spirit and attitude of gratitude. Work to keep it going in your life too.

Good & Plenty Worksheet

Instructions: Fill in the table as follows - in the column on the left list everything you have ownership, responsibility, and accountability for. This is a priority column. Your daily household and workplace tasks don't belong here. In the middle column fill in how you are fulfilling what you are called to do in the areas that coincide with the items on the left. Please don't limit yourself to the space provided. Write as much as you need to in the middle column. This exercise will assist in creating a snapshot of how you are doing in the area of stewardship. At the conclusion I hope it will be clear which areas have gaps and could use a little more attention from you. You'll capture this in the far right column. I've given you an example. Like in the chapter before, take your time and continue with those notes about what you are thinking and feeling as you go through this exercise. Hey, don't leave out your community. You live there along with everyone else, and if there are things you could be doing to assist your neighbors and fellow residents to help maintain or improve your quality of living and safety, then let's include that too.

I have ownership, responsibility and accountability for . . .	My specific actions to fulfill what I am called to do are . . .	I can improve stewardship in this area by . . .
My children	Provide a safe, loving home environment; good education; health coverage; family time; vacations; support their goals; help and assist when needed.	Spending more individual time with each of them.

I have ownership, responsibility and accountability for . . .	My specific actions to fulfill what I am called to do are . . .	I can improve stewardship in this area by . . .

I have ownership, responsibility and accountability for . . .	My specific actions to fulfill what I am called to do are . . .	I can improve stewardship in this area by . . .

Chapter 7:

FLOW – Feel Love Over Worry

———— ● ● ————

"You have brains in your head. You have feet in your shoes. You can steer yourself in any direction you choose."

DR. SEUSS

t should be obvious by now that I love the Lord, and that I try to include Him in every aspect of my life, including writing this book. I say "try to" because I am not perfect. I fall short like everyone else does at times. There is indeed a higher power orchestrating the events and circumstances in our lives and that having an attitude of gratitude can attract love and positivity. God is the Master Orchestrator. He is outstanding at putting the right people, in the right place, at the right time, under the right circumstances. He pricks hearts and causes people to move into action. He can turn what feels like an overwhelming and seemingly impossible situation around in an instant. That's if you let Him.

God expresses His love to us in many ways. One way is by giving each of us the freedom to choose. We get to choose whether to believe and love Him. We get to choose right from wrong. We get to choose to resist temptation or to be consumed by it. We get to choose to be forgiving or revengeful. We get to make our own choices in every aspect of our lives. The one thing about having the freedom to choose that folks get tangled up in is the consequences to some of the choices.

It was June 2010 when I was done, at my wits end, and decided that I had had enough. Remember in Chapter 1 when I mentioned that everything had pretty much gone to, you know what, in a handbasket? Well, June 2010 was one of those times. I started making moves – literally. I had decided to get trained and go on the road and drive a big rig. You're probably laughing right now, but it's true. I'd be on the road and gone for weeks at a time. Ha! Let's see how they get along without me then. How long will they last without Mom around? Who's gonna take care of everything and everyone? Oh well, not for me to worry about anymore. I'm hitting the road! I completed my application, paid my money, enrolled in a training class to get my certification, downloaded all my training materials, and was looking forward to my start date. Then, two weeks before I was going to let the front door hit me on my backside, I broke my leg, clean through.

Here's the story: On the second day of my family's visit with friends, we decided to go bowling. We arrived just as their local bowling alley opened their doors for the day. We were the first and only bowlers. The manager provided shoes for each of us, directed us to where to get our bowling balls, and assigned us two lanes. We set up teams and I was the first to bowl out of our group. Now remember, we were the first to arrive at the bowling alley, and I was the first to bowl for our team. I studied my target and walked slowing toward the lane. The instant I hit the boundary line, ready to release my ball, I slipped in such a way that I flew up into the air and landed in a way that instantly changed the course of my life.

My husband was by my side fairly quickly as I hadn't moved a muscle. The pain in my leg was about to cause me to pass out and my face was resting in a puddle of hot tears. He whispered in my ear with a chuckle in his voice, "I know you're embarrassed but you've got to get up now."

Fast-forward. The ambulance and paramedics arrived. One paramedic commented about the glob of oil right where I was lying. It was actually slippery and dangerous for them to work on me at that spot. Apparently, the lanes had been oiled and buffed right before the bowling alley opened. The oil at the base of the lane I was bowling on had not been spread, nor the lane buffed. Really! The one lane that had not been serviced was the lane I was to be the first to bowl on!

Why did it happen? I don't know about you, but in my life journey there have been times when God steps in and changes the direction where my life is headed. As the Master Orchestrator, he shifts things in my life in such a way that I end up exactly where He needs me to be. Sometimes the shift is not so gentle. Sometimes it can be painful.

I believe with all my heart that I was not supposed to be a big rig driver. I laugh at the thought today. I believe I was to keep my butt right at home, where I would continue to 'grow' through a sequence of circumstances and events. The break in my right leg was a clean one; straight through the bone. I would be in a cast for the next seven months and not permitted to put any pressure on the broken leg for at least five of the seven. I'm not suggesting that God only uses pain to get our attention or orchestrate our lives. He works differently in each of our lives and knows what will be most effective. The lessons I learned during those months were invaluable, and yes, I told my husband what I was planning and had secretly put in motion. He just looked at me and kissed me gently.

Life should definitely not happen to you. It should happen with you and for you. We should use that freedom to choose what God gave us to influence how our life unfolds. Allowing things to take shape in our lives when we can think and respond in a way that will produce positive life-affirming outcomes is certainly the way to go. I think of my community and the officers who sit on our home association board. These volunteers are riddled daily with complaints from community residents, yet these same residents don't want to volunteer, lend a hand to assist in any way, or even step up to run for any of the positions themselves. They just complain. If you want to see change in anything you have to be part of the effort and movement to do so.

I mentioned in the last chapter how important sharing is. In this chapter, I want to share another aspect of sharing, and that is the benefit of getting support and assistance from others. When we share our plans and intentions with others, we are more likely to get help to whatever end we are working toward. In a recent training I facilitated, I gave the example of being in the far-left lane on a four-lane highway and trying to move over to get off on the next exit. You try to move your car over, lane by lane, and it's difficult. Drivers are not letting you get into the lane. The transition from the far-left lane to the far-right lane becomes somewhat easier when you decide to let oncoming cars know your intentions, by simply putting on your right blinker. The same holds true with so much else in our lives. Most often our path to success includes the help and support of others. No one will know what we need and how they can help, if we don't share. Of course, we have to be wise and discerning when we do. Yes, I know, not everyone has our best interest at heart.

So there's power in choosing and power in sharing. There's also power in gratitude. Research reveals that gratitude opens the door to more and better relationships; improves physical health; improves psychological health; increases mental strength; enhances empathy, reduces aggression, and improves self-esteem. Grateful people even sleep better. I know that having a good night's sleep is always at the top of my wish list when I go to bed. There are many resources on the market to help you be more gracious in your daily life and in your dealings with others. If your current situation has sabotaged your ability to be grateful most, if not all of the time, then consider all of the amazing benefits research shows. Not enough? Well here's more: gratitude can make you happier and make you more attractive to others, and it strengthens your emotions and helps you to be more optimistic. Gratitude is not a cure-all, but there's plenty of research to support the claims, and power in it when we exercise it. Gratitude is an underutilized tool for improving life satisfaction and happiness.

Here's another power that works for me. The power of a cool shower. Yes. A cool, refreshing shower. Not just for the obvious reasons. You know how good a shower feels after working out and sweating, or how good a shower feels after a long day at work. There's so much power in a shower. It relieves stress, speeds up muscle soreness and recovery, improves immunity and circulation, relieves depression, increases alertness, refines hair and skin, and even stimulates weight loss. Need more reasons to consider a cold shower a beneficial tool? Go to the internet.

Ever notice how much better things move along and seem to flow when you choose to feel love? I mean intentionally feel love when things and people make it hard. Intentionally replacing negative thoughts with loving ones; taking a deep breath and choosing to pause when you could respond in a way you might regret? How about when you choose the opposite? You fret. You worry. You're concerned. You feel anxious and apprehensive, and then undoubtedly you attract more of whatever it is you're feeling negative about. Again, it's all a choice. Choosing the high road with its pleasant and positive responses; now that takes practice. Practice. Practice. Practice.

When you know better you do better; at least most of the time. Right? I remember the day I wanted to share an idea with my hubby. This idea would mean he'd have to be an active part in it and do something. On this day, I was hoping he and I could agree on a plan that would change some of the negative behaviors our oldest was displaying. Now, I need you to recall the story about how my husband allowed my daughter to leave the house after midnight, after I had clearly told her she couldn't. The dynamic between the two was such where I was apparently the enemy. You know, the person who has high expectations of everyone and expects that each person will take responsibility and be accountable for their actions? That's the enemy. That's how I felt at the time. Anyway, I could have easily felt anxious about his response to my idea, and it would have been quite natural for me to, given the dynamic and how long it existed, but instead I chose to feel the love I have for him and for my daughter. It was so much easier, and so hubby and I sat and talked. He was open and listened with an open and loving heart. I believe this had everything to do with my own words being kind and loving. One of my favorite scriptures, 1 Corinthians 13, verse 7 says, "Love bears all things, believes all things, hopes all things, endures all things." Choosing to flow – feel love over worry worked very well that day, and he and I agreed, very happily I might add, on a plan to help our daughter. The plan didn't work. However, that's not the point for today.

Personal Prescription

Building confidence leads to success in most every area of your life. You can empower yourself and here are a few steps to get you on your way: Stop putting other people on a pedestal. When you do this you may begin to believe that what they are doing or what they have is not achievable for you, and this is just not true. Cultivate your relationship with fear. Fear is not a bad thing on its own. It's when we match our thoughts and actions to it that it becomes a problem and can paralyze us. Step into it and act in spite of it. Develop positive beliefs. Keep in mind that your beliefs are our lenses into how we see the world. We can practice being positive and developing positive beliefs. Practice like you would the favorite thing you like to do. Take action. Taking action creates the bridge you will need to get from where you are to where you want to go. Action can take your dreams to becoming a reality. You, not anyone else, are responsible for the life you create through your actions.

FLOW Worksheet

Instructions: Fill in the table as follows - in the column on the left list a sequence of events that ultimately resulted in you being connected to something or someone you needed to be connected with or to; you being kept safe; a significant life lesson; or any experience that you feel strongly was orchestrated by God. In the column in the middle fill in how you responded as things were unfolding. In the column on the far right capture what the result/outcome was to the sequence of events or experience, in the left-hand column. As always, take your time and really be reflective here. There are obvious ways God is working in our lives and most other ways are considerably less obvious. Reflective practice is, in its simplest form, thinking about or reflecting on an experience and how you responded, and that perhaps you decided to learn from it and possibly do something different the next time.

Experience	How you responded	Result/Outcome
Had enough; enrolled in big rig school; broken leg	Emotional at first, followed by frustration, then obediently still	Amazing lesson in being able to receive love and support.

Experience	How you responded	Result/Outcome

Chapter 8:

The Feeling Machine

●—●

"Let me give up the need to know why things
happen as they do. I will never know and constant
wondering is constant suffering."

CAROLINE MYSS

What parent would ever imagine having to visit their child in jail? What parent would ever imagine losing their child to a drug overdose? What parent would ever imagine their child being anything other than a good, contributing member of society?

In the past few years, I've met a number of women who lost their son or daughter to an opioid overdose. I met a police officer who shared the story of his daughter with me. His daughter got mixed up with the wrong crowd, and before anyone knew, became addicted to drugs. She was doing things this police officer dad could have never imagined his sweet, smart, and talented daughter would do. He tried to pull her from that life. Being a police officer didn't give him special powers or some special skill the rest of us could not have access to. He tried all he knew how to do, and still felt helpless until the day he received the call that she had overdosed and died.

I've met men and women who are dealing with the fact that their child is in prison now. You are devastated to get the call, yet feelings of frustration and anger creep in to justify your thoughts of leaving them there in hopes of teaching them a lesson. The immature behavior and poor choices need to stop. You want them to feel loved, yet the image you never want to have in your head is one where they are behind bars. So, you delay your visit, or you don't go at all. You just pay their bail, so you can get them home – quickly – where it's safe. I found myself there, in that mental space of trying to decide what would be best for my oldest daughter; running around with the wrong crowd, and carelessly, needlessly, making choices that would put her in harm's way. What would produce the best, desired outcome? Who in the world knows the right answer? In situations like this, we are very driven and motivated by our feelings, and I don't believe this is a good thing.

Feelings. It's important to recognize them for what they are, but first let's consider what they are not. Feelings are not facts and just because at some point in time you may feel helpless or hopeless, it doesn't mean that you are either. Feelings can be awfully unreliable and uncontrollable at times. Joyce Meyer was quoted as saying, "Our feelings are unreliable and cannot be trusted to convey truth." Yet, we are feeling machines! We do have to be discerning. While on the one hand, feelings are considered unreliable, there are certainly situations when they might give important signals. A bad conscience might indicate some wrongdoing, and fear might signal danger. This is not, however, significant enough to trust feelings unconditionally. Most of us know that when emotions are high, it's not a good time to make big, life-changing decisions. Remember me and the big rig? When emotions are high your judgement is clouded, and it becomes difficult to focus. The more emotional you feel, the less logical your thoughts will be. We know that the best, most reliable decisions are based on facts and not feelings. But what about the feelings invoked by our children? Our significant others? Our jobs?

Decisions, decisions. There are a number of ways to improve your ability to make sound decisions and for them to become a habit in every aspect of your life. Here's a simple approach. It will sound more business-like than everyday life-like, but the skill, which can become habit, is transferable. Start with your desired outcome. This is classic Stephen Covey Habit #2 Begin with the End in Mind. This means to begin with a clear vision of your desired destination, then continue by flexing your proactive muscles to make things happen. Second, rely on quality data and valuable insights. Doing this helps your decision-making to become more scientific and provides more control on outcomes. When my daughter found herself in trouble, I had to get the specifics and facts about what happened, to fully understand the situation so I could make the most appropriate decision about next steps. Third, you may want to use a S.W.O.T. analysis. It's a great decision-making tool, and not just for business, I assure you. If you've never seen this acronym before it stands for strengths, weaknesses, opportunities, and threats. It's ideal in helping you identify key issues that may have significant impact on the decisions you need to make. A S.W.O.T. analysis does not, however, offer solutions. Fourth, visualize and simulate the possible outcomes. This may come from experience, business acumen, and a clear understanding of who all the decision will impact. I often sit and contemplate the various ways a situation can play out, depending on how I decide to engage. Lastly, trust your instincts. You can call it your gut feeling, your intuition, whatever you'd like. Some of the world's greatest leaders rely on their intuition to make some tough decisions, and they swear by it. I think your intuition is one of those things that people can use every day, but underestimate its power when it comes to making decisions.

When I first moved to Atlanta, I visited quite a few churches before finding the church home that I still attend today. I recall one of the pastors gave a sermon on the consequences of letting your feelings dictate your actions. He told a story of a man who left his house in plenty of time to get to work on time. Being on time was critical for this man because he had been given a warning that being late even one more day would result in him being terminated. Unfortunately, there was an accident that caused a great deal of traffic on the expressway this particular morning. Traffic had pretty much come to a halt. He fretted as his car, and hundreds of others, sat idle in what was now a parking lot on the expressway. As the minutes passed, he become more and more anxious and frustrated. These feelings got the best of him and he decided to get out of the car. At this point, he was sure to be late for work. In his frustration, he began cursing at no one in particular. A father who had his children in the car next to his did not appreciate his behavior and asked him to stop. The man, over-the-top with frustration and consumed by emotion, directed his negative energy to the father. One thing led to another and before you know it, a policeman on motorcycle pulled up. The man was so out of control at this point that the policeman had to call for backup, and ultimately arrested the man. As his feelings dictated, the man never made it to work and so lost his job. He ended up losing his wife as well that day.

Why, you ask? Losing this job would be the sixth job the man has lost in the past year, and his wife had had enough. She made it clear just the week before that she was giving him this one last chance to keep a job and turn things around financially for their family. If not, she was taking the kids and going to live with her parents. The man's bail was set for $600. He was also faced with the fees associated with having his car removed from the scene. Everyone in the congregation got the message the pastor was trying to convey. How much power do we give our feelings, and how critical is it that we don't give up control to them? I got the message as well but I couldn't help but wonder what would have happened if the man had only called his job and asked his boss to look at the news. I bet his boss would have seen a report of the accident. The accident and resulting traffic could certainly have been verified in some way. I'd like to believe the boss would have made an exception for the man being late on this day. Like I said in Chapter 1, I can't judge. I have quite a few examples of letting my emotions get the best of me. I have even more examples of my oldest daughter allowing her feelings and emotions to get the best of her, which resulted in a number of situations where my husband and I have had to rescue her from herself.

Yes. Rescue my daughter from herself. I would always tell her and countless other young women that their words, actions, and behaviors will always tell the world how to treat them. That feelings of high self-worth and self-confidence are important aspects of being their healthiest and best self.

Every time we speak, we get to choose the words we use. Every time we respond to anything, we get to decide how and what it looks like, especially to others. If every time we have a project we find ourselves dilly-dallying and putting things off until the last minute, we most likely have a habit of procrastination. This does not mean that we are procrastinators. We just have the habit. We don't feel like getting started. We don't feel like being mindful. We don't feel like this or that. Whatever it is, it is driven by our feelings! Developing new, positive, life-affirming habits are not easy, especially with the fact that the habits we formed during our formative years become harder and harder to shake as time moves forward. It's not impossible, just harder.

So, what do we do? How do we even begin? This is going to sound like a contradiction, but we need to start with a feeling, a very powerful one. You know what I'm talking about. The feeling you get when the doctor tells you that you will die if you don't lose weight. How instantly motivated you are to diet and exercise so you can be around a little longer for your loved ones. Yes! You do want to be at your children's weddings and be around to see and enjoy your grandchildren. That feeling right there when your boss puts you on warning that if you don't improve your work performance, you will be fired. That fight or flight feeling that you must respond or do something to change the situation. Yes. Fight or flight. For some people it is a terrifying thought to lose their spouse, their job, their reputation, whatever is important enough to motivate them into action. If you don't feel the power of the feeling generated by the thought of losing something or someone, or the feeling generated by the fact that an unwanted situation will result if you don't do something to change the possibility of it occurring, it will be very difficult to develop new, good, sustainable habits.

I had a women's heart screening at my local hospital recently. I made the appointment when I was reminded that heart disease is the leading cause of death in women, and that the symptoms almost always go unnoticed. Praise God that all my results came back negative, but it was the feeling I got when the doctor said to me: "Whatever you're doing, keep doing it" that fueled my workouts, my desire to make better food choices, and my motivation to schedule regular and consistent opportunities to do something fun and relaxing. It sounds crazy but I'm looking forward to hearing the doctor say those words to me again next year. Sounds like a new, good, sustainable habit in the works.

So, like the unfortunate situation the man on the expressway found himself in on his way to work that dreadful morning, what do you do when things don't go the way you planned? Perhaps you allowed your feelings to dictate your responses and now you feel some regret. OK, maybe you don't feel regret, but you recognize you could have handled things differently – better even. When we create an undesired outcome, we don't have to feel condemned by it; we can feel some conviction, acknowledge it, and use the experience for a better outcome the next time around. Period. Every time your mind wants to replay it, acknowledge it and replace it with the visual of the better outcome for next time, make sure there's an equally positive feeling to accompany it. Practice. Practice. Practice.

Personal Prescription

I went to visit my oldest daughter's high school counselor during her junior year. I was asking for advice, as well as her thoughts on the behavior and recent choices my daughter had been making. This counselor had a kind face and super sweet disposition. She listened to me then shared some of what she'd seen and experienced in her 30-plus years as a school guidance counselor. She'd talk to a countless number of parents like me. She ended our talk with these words of advice: "Just love her through it." It's not been easy, but that's what I've been doing from the very beginning. When you can't figure it out, when you have days that are tougher than others, choose to love anyway. The next day is a new day – a chance to try again, – and to love some more.

The Feeling Machine Exercise

Instructions: Find a space where you can be alone and where it will be quiet for at least 20 minutes. If you feel a strong urge to write things down while going through this mental exercise, please do. Ideally, I'll want you to capture your thoughts and feelings at the end, but I don't want anything to keep you from going through this exercise fully. Consider just one thing, a situation or circumstance that you are dealing with, in your life currently. It needs to be the thing that will require you to engage in, to do something. Mentally inventory the facts surrounding the thing you've chosen. All the facts please, even the ones that don't support your agenda. Consider the possible ways you might engage or respond. Play out in your mind each possible way you might engage or respond and what the outcome would be for each. If you've reflected on three different ways, then there should be three difference scenarios being played out in your mind. One at a time with a defined beginning and end. Don't rush. Now here's the key – it's important to recognize and acknowledge what you are feeling as you play out each scenario.

_____

_____

_____

_____

_____

_____

_____

_____

_____

_____

_____

_____

_____

_____

_____

_____

_____

_____

_____

_____

_____

_____

Chapter 9:

The Business of YOU

———●—●———

"Let today be the day you give up who you've been for who you can become."

HAL ELROD

The work I did with my first two clients lasted for as long as it needed to. It wasn't about anything but "progress" for both. There certainly was a fair share of hills and valleys in their journey process, but we weathered every storm and celebrated every milestone together. It was awesome for me to be part of their journey and ultimately their respective victories over the areas of their lives that needed a makeover – "overhaul" is more like it. The times that stick out most for me have everything to do with doubt, worry, and frustration. They had achieved mastery at forming some level of doubt and reasons to worry about everything, and I do mean everything!

Well, we worked diligently through a process to short-circuit this inclination. Some of the behavior was what came natural for them, and some of it was being conditioned as a result of a series of similar life experiences spanning over an extended period of time. Despite the hard work and challenges associated with creating real and lasting change,

I was super excited for them. How could I not be? They were embarking upon a journey that would allow them to transcend the dynamics of their home life, their ability to impact the culture in which they work, as well as their ability to contribute in their communities in a meaningful way. It was an honor and blessing for me to be there the day the lightbulb turned on for them, the same way it did for me. Both clients are experiencing an amazing new life, fearless and equipped to do "that thing" God called them to do.

The road to an amazing new life is narrow, but room enough for both of us. The road is narrow because it is rarely traveled and meant only for those who are ready to engage and commit to seeing the process through to the end. Get this: Science says that a whopping 98 percent of people die without ever fulfilling their dreams. Staggering! That grieves me. When something resonates with you, write it down. When something evokes emotion within you, write it down. It's an important part of the process to go back and reflect on some of these things. Thinking, dreaming, wanting, wishing, and whatever other "-ing" you can think of, will never do what the action called doing can help you to achieve. There are many, many reasons why people don't follow through with their plans, their goals, and their desires for a richer, more meaningful life. Whatever the reasons, they can all be overcome with the proper tools and strategies.

I am instantly reminded of a day back fourteen years ago. It was the anniversary of the day when I had moved from New York to Georgia just one short year before. The kids and I were still adjusting to country life, my adjustment being a little longer and more difficult, and settling into our newly built home. My husband was still working in New York, us both with the hope that he would retire in just two short years. Fortunately for us, we have a wonderful, extended family relationship that came with flight benefits at the time, and so my husband could travel home to Georgia each week on his days off. My kid's dad never missed a birthday, holiday, concert, school play, or anything of significance during this time of what I call transition.

On this particular day, my husband's flight to Georgia was scheduled to land on time and my brother-in-law was going to pick him up for me. I was about to burst with excitement about my plans to share with him my idea for what would be the next big thing I was going to do. I say the next big thing because I had enjoyed some fairly big things thus far. A successful tour of duty in the United States Air Force. Significant success in my corporate career. Started two businesses and acquired a beautiful home in both New York and now in Georgia. Lots of travel abroad and good friends to enjoy good times with was the sweet topping. Leaving my corporate job was a big step and I believed that the appropriate next step was to launch a new business. To kick-start it off, I would allow the author in me to make her big reveal. I had the storyline ready as well as the business plan and the business strategy that would follow.

My hubby walked through the door and as soon as he gave the last of our three children a kiss and hug, I was in his face with my exciting news. He smiled while I shared and unfolded my plan at one hundred miles an hour. When I was done, I searched his face for mutual excitement and love. Instead there was a sweet smile followed by an "OK." He then turned and walked away. Not in any disrespect. He'd heard what I said and simply moved on. I stood there however, stiff, with my jaw agape, for at least 30 seconds as I watched him walk into my sister's kitchen. The only thing I can say about me that day is that something happened. Something changed in my mind and in my spirit. You may be reading this and thinking that I moved on and executed my plan anyway, but I didn't. Instead, I folded in half the papers I had printed about publishing, and my business plan, and tucked them in my leather organizer. There those papers sat, year after year, until I finally threw them away in 2013.

Yes. You read it right. For nine years, I carried around that dream– literally. Each year I would change the calendar insert in my organizer from the old year to the New Year, and each year I would look at the papers absentmindedly, and then tuck them back in the organizer the same way. By now you must be thinking that my husband is not a very nice man, inconsiderate even, but the complete opposite is true. Yes, I was looking for a very different response that day, a little encouragement and mutual excitement. While he is an awesome and loving person, he and I are not the same in how we think and how we respond, and he's also human. To this day, I don't have a name for what happened to me on that day, or why I physically carried this particular dream around in my leather organization for nine years. All I know is that the lessons I learned in the journey from that day until now have been incredible. Lessons I've been able to share with my clients. Lessons that have changed and influenced their lives in significant ways.

So, let's do a little excavating, if you will, and please bear with me. If we can't always explain why we do or say what we do and say, then how can we expect to always be able to explain this behavior in others? You raised your child with a certain endgame in mind. More than likely it had everything to do with graduating, going to college, and then landing a great-paying job. Possibly even starting a business of their own or beginning an apprenticeship relationship to take over yours. Whatever the plan, it most likely did not include them still being at home. I bet it also didn't include them draining your finances well after high school or college graduation. So why then? While us parents aren't one hundred percent responsible for this behavior, we do however, have some behaviors we absolutely have to look at – especially if we're still doing some unintentional things that may be contributing, in even the smallest of ways, to our current situation.

Stick with me. My son, a college graduate, drives a BMW. Yes, we gave it to him. My son has a job and does well for a young man fresh out of school. One day his car started acting up and he decided it needed to go in the shop. He shared his plans with my husband and asked if there was another car he could use. "If there was another car he could use?" Does anyone other than me see the problem in this statement? There are families who have to share just one car, families who have no car and have to take public transportation. This young man is looking for the keys to one of the other cars in our garage. This is not a mindset my son created. It's a mindset and conditioning my husband and I created, and I own it *&^%! This conversation between my son and my husband continued with my husband explaining that he wouldn't have a problem letting our son drive one of the other cars but, at that time, one needed a battery and another was in the shop. I couldn't take it another minute. What happened to asking for a ride? Granted, we don't live in a community that has public transportation, but really? The first thought is to get the keys to another car? I interjected and offered to give my son a ride to work whenever I could, and suggested that he check in with friends to get help as well. I don't know how the conversation would have turned if I suggested he ride one of the bikes in the garage. Ha. Fast forward, my son got by with a little help from his friends. His car was in the shop only a few days – what an inconvenience. Not!

You know what just popped into my mind? The day my oldest daughter was around seven years old and my sister was watching her for me, along with my older sister's kids, after school. When she dropped my daughter off at home that night, she told me that when she asked all the kids what they wanted for an after-school snack, everyone except my daughter screamed for peanut butter and jelly sandwiches. My daughter asked for salmon.

Does that have anything to do with my daughter? You bet it doesn't! If we parents don't recondition our thinking, behaviors and habits, we may find ourselves dealing with many more challenges and for a much longer time. We can decide to stop at any time. Yeah, I know, most of the damage – I mean conditioning – has been done, but you know what? We need to give our adult children, the ones who are dealing with laziness or unwillingness, and oh, is it safe to say, being spoiled, a chance to figure things out. I mean what if you stopped exceeding your food budget? What if you stopped paying for their insurance and their phone bill? How long do you really think that one of today's young adults will go without a phone? Ok, what if you simply stopped giving them "pocket money" because you feel bad that he or she doesn't have a job? Are you giving them money for gas, too? Wait! What? Did you just think to yourself: "Well, how can they look for a job and then get to work if I don't pay for their insurance?" Did you really just think that? Why don't you try it and see? What did you do when you were that age? I'm sorry, was that too brash? Please forgive me. Sometimes I get very – passionate. But try it. Give them a chance. If you just stop, or say no, your adult child may figure it out. You'll know when and how best to help and support them when, and if, you need to. I don't know, maybe you and I didn't grow up the same. My parents didn't help me through school. They didn't purchase a car for me or pay any of my bills at any time. Of course, our parents love us, but my husband and I both had to work hard and figure things out. Suffice it to say, my home is a comfortable place. Is it possible that I've made living, I mean staying, at home easy and a little too comfortable?

One of my clients has an adult child living at home. When she and I first talked, she shared with me how absolutely disgusting his room was, and that her grocery bill had doubled since he decided to leave college after two years and come home. We addressed and took care of both of those matters right away. Her son is still living at home, but his room stays clean and my client does not exceed her budget for groceries. He's since gotten a job, enough to contribute some groceries to the household. In this solution, my client needed to change and do some things differently. Her son is making great progress. Speaking of sons, I remember the day my son accused me of buying less food since he came home from college. What's even more ridiculous than his comment is that he never recognized that he eats more today than when he left for college, and that I did increase my budget for groceries, but there is a threshold. Fortunately, he understood better after we spoke. He's thoughtful, has a job, and has no problem purchasing extra groceries for himself when his body's metabolism kicks into overdrive.

So much of what we do, what our adult children do, and what our spouses do, is rooted in fear. We've over-parented and the world today is a seemingly unfriendly place. Our adult children are young, and we've handed so much to them over the years, that expecting them to leave the nest willingly and with confidence is a bit of a stretch and may take more effort on our part than we expected. I get concerned when I hear parents of young children boast about kicking their children out of the house as soon as the child turns 18. Apparently that's what their parents did to them, and after all, they turned out ok.

I'd be remiss if I didn't mention the dynamic of companionship. If by chance you are a parent who doesn't realize you are using your child for companionship or emotional support, please consider some self-reflection. In an article written by long-time therapist Kathy Hardie-Williams, she shares that many times when she is working with people who are developmentally stuck, they end up sharing that, as children, they were the person their parent turned to as a confidant or for emotional support. Children put in this position may feel special or privileged because the parent is sharing adult information with them and/or is looking to them for support, creating a sense of closeness. However, given that the child's needs are ignored in favor of the parent's, there can be devastating long-term developmental consequences. Clearly, it is desirable for parents and their children to be close. However, in healthy parent-child relationships, parents prioritize their children's emotional needs as opposed to children taking care of the parent's emotional needs. When children are put in the position of meeting the emotional needs of a parent, it creates an unhealthy dynamic in which children essentially become the parents. The children are emotionally abandoned, in effect robbing them of their childhood.

Personal Prescription

So what happens when you try something new and it doesn't work? You try again, right? Not always. Some people internalize failure as incompetence. They are instantly demotivated. They don't realize that it's just one experiment that was not successful, and there could very well be many more before something takes hold and actually works. It's imperative that you push forward and try again even if you're uncomfortable, and even if it's the same thing you need to try. Perhaps the right conditions, thoughts and feelings included, were not in place for that thing to have worked on whatever day you chose. Jonathan Mildenhall was quoted as saying: "If you don't have room to fail, you don't have room to grow." So, keep growing and keep things moving. Try again, and as many times as necessary until you achieve your desired outcome.

The Business of YOU

Instructions: Answer the questions. Please be as thoughtful and as thorough as you can. This is not an exercise to see how bad, guilty, or ashamed we can make you feel about anything you've done while raising your children. No way. We all are doing the best job we can. Please trust me. There is value in looking at how we've contributed to some things, so we can change our mindset and develop the kinds of habits and behaviors that will fare us, and those we love, much better.

1. What did you regularly do for your children that they should have done for themselves?
2. What did you give to your children that they should have worked hard for and earned?
3. What did you give to your children that they could have done without or was a little excessive?
4. In what ways have you conditioned your children to respond to you?

Chapter 10:

Personal Power

— ● ● —

*"Your work is to discover your world,
and then with all your heart give yourself to it."*
GAUTAMA BUDDHA

I was simply exhausted on this August Friday. Simply exhausted. I had a long and somewhat stressful day at work and was feeling overwhelmed by the fact that my book club was meeting at my house that evening. The house needed cleaning and all I could reflect on from leaving the house that morning was how messy the kitchen was. A headache began a slow beat on the right side of my head, right above my eye. As I drove home, I tried to mentally strategize how I would make the most out of the hour and a half I had before my fellow book lovers would arrive. I wouldn't even have time to change from my work clothes into something more casual and comfortable.

As I pulled into my garage, the headache was suddenly accompanied by a sinking feeling that got deeper as I realized, I forgot to stop by the store to pick up something sweet for the group to enjoy. I was done. Mentally. And. Physically. When I walked into the house I was hit instantly with the smell of clean. You know what that smells like in your home.

The smell that says everything is in its place and everything's in order. The smell that says things got moved and dusted behind. Things got lifted, swept, and mopped. The smell of dryer sheets and the smell of clean with a hint of citrus. I was also hit with the look of shine. You know that, too. Everything is shiny and glistening like it's brand new. Oh, and that's not all. There was the smell of something sweet; something fresh baked. I was in the twilight zone, and I was so overwhelmed that my eyes instantly began to burn with tears. I continued to walk further into the house and allowed my eyes, and nose, to take it all in. There was a tray of homemade brownies, sprinkled with confectioners' sugar sitting on the super shiny kitchen counter. Right then, my oldest daughter came out of the bathroom and greeted me with a hello and a kiss. She asked if I was OK, because at that point, my eyes were glossy with tears. I told her that I was fine. More than fine and expressed my appreciation for all she had done to get me prepared for the evening. She told me that she knew that with work and all, it would be hard for me to get everything ready, and so she wanted to help. Her eyes gave me the once over and suggested I get changed and freshened up.

I hope I described this story well enough for you to understand how major that was for me. It was an expression of love toward me, for me, and it was powerful. I didn't ask for help. I didn't say a thing. I didn't make a call or send a text. When you get that unexpected expression of love, in whatever way speaks to you, it can fill your love tank to full. In an instant, you are overflowing with love yourself and you are energized and motivated to carry it forward.

Carolyn Myss is one of my favorite authors. In her book, Invisible Acts of Power: Personal Choices That Create

Miracles, she asks and responds to these questions: What are the long-range consequences that result from even the smallest favors offered to others? What really takes place in the energetic field of life when someone responds to someone else in need? Carolyn Myss does an outstanding job explaining why being of service to another person is not an option. It is a biological necessity. I had a need that day, and my daughter rose to the occasion. There are many ways that you and I can create small, yet profound miracles, gain a greater sense of spirit, and transform your life and that of others in an instant. All it takes is an act of kindness, from the heart. Here's one smaller example of an invisible act of power: It had to be somewhere around 9 p.m. on a week night and I was still at the office. There was a knock at my office door, and there she was, my oldest daughter with a number 1 from Chick-fil-A in one hand, and a lemonade in the other. Out of nowhere. In an instant. Things change.

By the way, do you know your love language? Do you know what a love language is? It's the way you receive love and feel love most significantly. When you understand your love language and the love language of your spouse and other family members, it's an incredibly powerful tool that can transform lives and certainly relationships. When you express love to others in their love language, amazing and powerful things happen. The concept of "love languages" was developed by Dr. Gary Chapman. In his book, The 5 Love Languages: The Secret to Love That Lasts, Dr. Chapman explains the five love languages, which are: Words of Affirmation is all about vocally affirming your loved ones; Acts of Service simply means that actions speak louder than words; Receiving Gifts is giving gifts to your loved ones, even little ones are a special expression of love; Quality Time is all about undivided, dedicated attention; and Physical Touch is pretty self-explanatory. Given the two examples I gave about the things my daughter did for me, you might think my love language is acts of service, but it's not. My primary love language is quality time, and my secondary love language is words of affirmation. It was the time my daughter took and dedicated to doing something special for me that spoke to me so powerfully.

When I worked for Deloitte, I attended a training called Exploring Group Dynamics by Kenneth Sole. It was one of the best professional and personal development trainings I've ever attended – second only to Stephen Covey's Leadership Training. It was challenging. No. It was hard and it stretched me for sure. I can't get into the particulars of it all. It would be time well spent if you ever get the opportunity to experience it for yourself. One thing I can share is one of the aspects about me that I learned. In a group of any kind, whether it be a family group or work group, my silence, face, and body language are often more powerful than my words. Learning this about myself, in such a powerful way (my training group was full of strangers and I had to live and share meals with them for a week) forever changed the way I communicate and interact with others. I am aware of how, through my communication style, I can impact a group or individual. I am aware of how powerful I am, and I want you to recognize the power within you and how you can positively, or negatively, impact others.

I am reminded of how elephants, one of the largest, most powerful, and exceptionally smart animals on earth, are conditioned from the time they are young. A circus elephant is trained by chaining them in infancy. Since the babies are not strong enough to pull free, they grow tired of trying and resign themselves to a life of limitations. They adapt to living in the boundaries set by the chain. As they grow through being conditioned in this way, after some time even a small rope is enough to restrain an enormous elephant. When you see an elephant at the circus standing behind what looks like a super short, wooden fence, don't you ever wonder why they don't just walk over, or through the fence and escape to freedom? You and I have talked about barriers and conditioning. Now we are talking about power, and like this elephant, you and I both are more powerful than we know today. We've identified our barriers and don't have to live within the boundaries created by others or the way we've been conditioned. There are so many ways to engage our power, and we can start by adding small, invisible acts of power, to our faith.

Some Christian musicians include the phrase, "I am a victor, not a victim" in their song lyrics, and you may hear this phrase used when Christians want to encourage each other during difficult circumstances. This is an interpretation of a part of the Bible that speaks quite a bit about our victory in Christ, and I stand on His word. It's true though, we are not victims, especially of our circumstances. God did not create us as such. If you've been paying attention and doing the work, you know whether you have a victim mentality. If this is the case, we've got to shift our mindset toward the truth about your power and greatness. You are not meant for a mundane or mediocre life. Jeremiah 29:11 says, "For I know the plans I have for you," declares the Lord, "plans to prosper you and not to harm you, plans to give you hope and a future." Let's get to it! Here's a little story of something I manifested through my inner power. OK, so I didn't plan for this to happen, but it manifested anyway because of the energy, words, and actions I put out into the universe.

My husband and I creatively use the traditional and modern wedding anniversary theme list to get gift ideas for whatever anniversary year we are celebrating. Musical instruments was the theme for the 24th wedding anniversary. We both enjoy putting our own creative spin on whatever the theme is and surprising each other with thoughtful gifts. The musical instruments theme was a little challenging. My husband doesn't play an instrument, and he has never shown a special interest in the sounds from any particular one. When the three months before our anniversary date turned into three weeks, I started feeling a little anxious. If whatever gift I decided upon needed to be ordered, I'd have to do it soon in order for it to arrive in time for our special day. One night it came to me. On our wedding day, hubby and I danced to Meli'sa Morgan's "You're All I Got."

Believe it or not, someone walked away with our Meli'sa Morgan CD on our wedding day, and we were never able to find it or replace it. We looked everywhere and searched the internet in hopes of finding a copy as well. We were willing to pay top dollar for our favorite CD, which also had our first dance wedding song. My bright idea was to try to locate the artist on Facebook and share our story. I was hoping that I could at least get her PR person to respond, and perhaps even get a replacement CD. Well, Meli'sa Morgan wasn't as hard to find as I thought she'd be. I sent her a private message with the details of my story. I even went as far as to ask her if she was planning to perform anytime soon, and where. She responded the very next day! Meli'sa Morgan responded to my message and I couldn't share this awesome news with my husband

– at least not until our anniversary anyway. The artist with the sultry voice was kind and congratulated us on the special occasion. She didn't offer a CD or anything, not even a poster. It was however very special to hear from the artist whose song we danced to on our wedding day. When three weeks turned to just three days before our anniversary, my back was against the wall. I recruited my son, who is incredibly talented. I ended up putting together a list of our favorite love songs from twenty-four years ago, so my son could put them on a CD. In addition, my son graphically designed a card that looked exactly like Casey Kasem's top 20 Billboard hits, and we listed the top 5 songs on the front of it. My husband loved it! The story doesn't end there. So you know that I reached out to Meli'sa Morgan without my husband's knowledge, for our 24th wedding anniversary. Well, an entire year goes by and it's time to celebrate our 25th wedding anniversary. The silver anniversary. A very special milestone for any couple; especially these days. A friend of my husband's sent him a text asking if he'd like to purchase tickets to a concert. A concert to be held in April, our anniversary month. You know what's coming – wait for it – a Meli'sa Morgan concert! Of course my husband said yes. We get to the concert to celebrate our anniversary, and not only does Meli'sa Morgan come off the stage to party with the audience, she takes a photo with hubby and me. The very next day she sends a Facebook private message to me to say how much she enjoyed meeting us and to thank us for being fans. How wonderful is that! It took a year to unfold, but that's how it was supposed to be. A perfect celebration of our 25th wedding anniversary. Celebrating and taking photos with the artist whose song we danced to for our first dance as

Mr. & Mrs. Reid. My energy, my thoughts, and my actions had everything to do with that manifestation. Powerful!

If you decide to check out Meli'sa Morgan's song, You're All I Got, you might also want to check out I Have Learned to Respect the Power of Love, a song by Stephanie Mills. I haven't heard it in months and it's been playing in my head over and over, while writing this chapter to you. Look it up. It's pretty awesome.

Below is the link to The 5 Love Languages Profile. Once you identify your love language, consider having your spouse and your children take the test as well. Once everyone knows their love language, everyone can work toward expressing love to each other in the way that will resonate best with each individual family member. Never compromise on your love language, and don't be shy about reminding those you love which language is yours.

Personal Prescription

Your personal power is your personal prescription to change your life and that of others. Gratitude sticks and any small act of kindness can resonate in your life or someone else's, for a lifetime. It's about doing something for someone that they are not expecting. You know how you feel when someone does something kind for you that you were not expecting. In addition to the kindness of my daughter, I remember the first time I pulled up to the window at a local Starbucks to pay for my order. The woman at the window told me that the person in the car in front of me had paid for my order. I didn't know the person in the car in front of me, but what that person did lifted my spirit in such a way that I couldn't help but smile and express kindness to others all throughout the day. I won't forget that kind gesture and the power it has to instantly change a mood, attitude, or situation.

Discover Your Love Language

http://www.5lovelanguages.com/profile/

The Shift

Chapter 11:

Let's Do Better

———•——•———

"If a man does not keep pace with his companions,
perhaps it is because he hears a different drummer.
Let him step to the music which he hears,
however measured or far away."

HENRY DAVID THOREAU

had the opportunity recently to connect with a dear friend whom I hadn't seen for at least two years. We talked and we talked. Then we talked some more. We hugged and we cried. We laughed and we squealed as we caught up on the ups and downs of the past two years of our lives. During our time together my friend shared that her son was not working, and that he was still not making the kind of decisions that would result in ideal outcomes. My friend shared that she had become exhausted by her son's lifestyle and the choices that would inevitably result in her having to come to his aid, and rescue, in some way. Her son had turned 40 years old the month prior to our meeting. Yes, you read it correctly, 40. I know that up to this point we've been talking about young adults, but the reality is that any adult, at any age, still living at home, can create a dynamic that causes a great deal of stress for everyone involved. Failure to launch is not a respecter of age.

I know my friend's son. I've known him since he was a little boy at the age of ten. I can recall, as he grew into a young man, many instances when he was incredibly helpful in assisting the older relatives in his family; especially when they were sick. As he grew older, his grandmother grew older and struggled quite a bit with her health. He chose to live with his grandmother and take care of her, for months at a time. My friend's son was amazing in how he lovingly and tenderly cared for his grandmother. How often do you see a young man willing to stay indoors, commit himself and care for a sick, elderly person? Not very often, I bet. I reminded my friend of this occasion and several others like it. She recalled those times with love and fondness, and then shared with me that her son had just recently taken care of one of his friend's older, sick relatives. That was it! That was her son's gift… his passion…taking care of seniors. He had worked many jobs during his adult life, and his time working in any of the jobs was never long. Interesting to note that not one of the jobs he's ever secured, was in the healthcare field. My friend became excited, and was suddenly on a mission to share with her son, thoughts about pursuing a career that involved helping and caring for seniors, during their time of need. Well, I'm happy to say that the conversation between mother and son did take place, and that her son has embarked upon a journey to pursue a caregiver certification. He's also got a job at an assisted-living facility. Yes! And this is only the beginning for him. I love happy endings.

I've mentioned the pleasure and joy I've experienced in working with young people and their families. I've learned so much about the millennial generation and how they impact those they live and work with. Despite the bad rap so many of them get, I find myself inspired by their creative mindset, and their unwillingness to get attached or stuck in anything that makes them feel uncomfortable, devalued or dissatisfied in any way. There have been countless jokes, videos and songs, all derogatory mind you, about millennials. When I hear people talk about how lazy they are, how they don't have a work ethic, or how they have an entitlement mentality, it pierces my heart and makes me cringe. It's not like I don't see, or haven't experienced some of the behaviors that are the brunt of many jokes and less than complimentary remarks, it's just that these young adults have so much more to offer than we seem willing to give them credit for. Let's not forget that they are our children, our young adults. They have specific ideals about how to work, when to work, and why the work they do should have meaning and benefit a cause of some sort, whenever possible.

As I work with parents, one of the messages I hear fairly consistently is about the expectations they have of their adult children. One father shared an incident where he demanded his oldest daughter make a plan for her life, then present it to him and his wife. The plan was to be complete and presented by the end of that week. Here's my concern: his daughter was set up to fail. The likelihood is that if she had a plan in the first place, writing it on paper or articulating it in some way to her parents, would have more than likely already been done. I know I haven't shared all the details about this particular situation, but what I can assure you is that this particular young adult did not need a demand or a deadline. What she needed at that time was guidance and encouragement;

especially from her parents. Not everyone has a plan, and most people, especially young adults, don't always know where to begin to create one. I know it's not intentional, but when we set up our young adults to fail, the outcome oftentimes results in a deeper, longer-lasting problem. This reminds me of a talk that Dandapani, international speaker and former monk, gave to a corporate business group. The topic was about focus. He asked the audience if they could recall how often, during their childhood, that their parents insisted they focus on their homework, or a specific task they were to complete. It seemed from the audience's response that they could recall, and everyone chuckled at the memories. The part of the talk that Dandapani wanted to highlight to his listeners was that no one, especially their parents, had ever taught them how to focus, but that they should just do it. This is not different from the plan the father expected of his daughter. We've got to do better, and it's not too late. It never is when it comes to helping our children.

This brings me to the matter of confidence. It doesn't exist in abundance in many young adults. For those of us who possess a good degree of confidence, we know that it is helpful, if not integral, to how we deal with the inevitable challenges of life. With confidence we believe in our abilities and personal strength. I'll add an extra layer for those of us who have confidence and trust in God; the author and finisher of our faith; the alpha and omega; the same yesterday, today, and forever. We know that there isn't anything too big for God, and so we experience and entertain fear less often. At least we try to. When young adults lack confidence and are not grounded in faith, they are less comfortable with themselves and therefore, more vulnerable to peer pressure and the demands of life. Confidence and self-esteem often go hand in hand. If your adult child has a low opinion of themself and lacks confidence in their abilities, making demands they are ill-equipped to handle, doesn't help the situation to progress in a positive direction. Negativity prevails in the form of derogatory self-talk, and isolation begins with being apprehensive about engaging with others, in healthy and meaningful ways. There is also an unwillingness to explore new and exciting opportunities. If you are fairly certain there is a confidence or self-esteem issue to be addressed, and are not sure how to go about doing so, consider some guidance and assistance from a professional, if it's within your means. I would. I believe it will be well-worth the time and money.

I know we all have stress, especially in this world of change and uncertainty. Here it is, we as parents have more experience and expertise to draw from when challenges come our way. Our adult children, the ones still living at home for all the reasons we've been discussing…not so much. If your adult child is on the younger side of the millennial-age spectrum, they most likely experience stress as "more stressful". Take this, and the fact that their prefrontal cortex, the part of the brain that assists with reasoning and controlling impulses, may not be fully developed. This has a large part to play in their inability to make the kind of decisions that could result in the best outcomes. There is most definitely a direct correlation between stress and poor decision-making in young adults. Actually, I know quite a few Generation Xers that this behavior exists in as well. So why do we put such emphasis on it when we see this behavior in our adult children?

Consider the number of people you know in your age group who are "stuck in a rut". They are those who seem to be able-bodied adults, yet they, like the adult children we've been focusing on, seem equally less motivated to do the things they need to do, in order to turn their life around. Tell me if any of these behaviors sound familiar in relation to your adult child: (1) day to day they don't seem motivated, perhaps doing quite a bit of sleeping; (2) they say they have ideas about doing something, they may even talk of a plan; (3) even though they may be doing some things, they are not doing the types of things necessary to shift their situation to a better direction; (4) they are never quite sure what day of the week it is; (5) if asked what they are doing or planning to do, the question is met with a less than positive response or the typical excuse. Well…I could go on, but the reality is, this same assessment is true for anyone who is stuck, not just our adult children. I highlight this similarity just to suggest, and hopefully encourage you, to think about the fact that if being stuck in a rut is challenging for us, our friends, peers, co-workers, you name it, imagine how incredibly challenging being lost and uncertain about the future must be for our adult children. I also believe that we, yes, you and I, have not done the best job in preparing our adult children for their successful entry into adulthood. I know I talked a little about this early on, so I won't beat a dead horse. I will however, talk about expressing love, God's love, to our adult children, until I'm blue in the face.

So, like we had to do when we were their age, our adult children have to establish an identity, build a foundation for the future, land a job, find a mate, repay student loans, pay bills, run errands, and whatever else "adulting" calls for. Doing these things does not automatically make for a successful and responsible adult. The stress of these expectations can lead to depression in any individual who lacks the ability to manage the details of life. I know it may start to sound like I'm making excuses for our adult children, but believe me when I say that I am not. What I know is that they need something we didn't need growing up, primarily because we were raised differently from the way we raised our children. I hope you know what I mean. No? Ok, so I'm the only one here who never received help with homework from their parents? Am I the only one who had to figure out a way to get home from practices and rehearsals, if I chose to join a team or play an instrument? Are you kidding? Am I the only one who had to figure out how to get a job? How to get a car? Well, what I know is that I not only helped my children with their homework; except for my son, who is brilliant and never asked me anything academic, I picked each of them up from practices, attended darn-near every concert, game, you name it, and then gave them each a car. Oh, and yes, if they didn't do so well in any competition, we celebrated the fact that they participated.

So what does this all mean? There's a very informative video on YouTube titled The Millennial Question featuring Simon Sinek. Within 15 minutes he shares what he believes are the four components that contribute to the state of mind and being for the millennial generation: parenting, technology, impatience and environment. The component I want to elaborate on is parenting. I could be embarrassed, but I'm not. I've grown past that. What I know is that everything I did for my children was motivated by love. If I had known better, I would have done better. In the video, Mr. Sinek talks about failed parenting strategies...the very ones my husband and I used. Yes, we told our children they could be anything they wanted to be and could have anything they wanted to have if they put their mind to it and worked hard. I have to admit, I still stand by this one. Yes, we advocated for our children in a way that ensured they were in the best schools and attended the classes with only the best teachers. Yes, we did pretty much everything he described. I have no regrets, and the reality is that all is well. I didn't always feel this way. I had to grow through the journey God would have me experience to get to a place where I can FLOW - Feel Love Over Worry, and to know that all is truly well.

So what do our adult children need that's different from past generations? They need us to help by filling in some gaps. Our adult children are part of a generation growing up with lower self-esteem than previous generations, through no fault of their own. They are thrust into the world after graduation, whether high school or college, and learn the hard way that they are not as special or as unique as they were raised and taught to believe. They are smacked in the face with the reality that their parents can't fix everything. They are totally blindsided by the fact that they can't have something just because they want it. Talk about the rug being pulled from under a person! The world of technology has provided an outlet to self-medicate, as well as an alternative to deep, meaningful relationships. Through social media, friends and followers can project an amazing life, all the while drowning and lost in a haze of depression. I recently shared a photo I took and gave it the name Digital Distraction. I included the following caption: "Because of the popularity of digital photography, dark rooms are not as popular as they once were. Because of the popularity of digital distractions, Jesus is not as popular as He once was." The social media platforms and smart phones our adult children immerse themselves in, have led to addictive behaviors for many. Who doesn't feel good when their posts get "likes"? What about the surge of endorphins when your number of friends and followers increase? We all receive a dose of dopamine when something feels good. If you're not familiar with it, dopamine is what some call the feel-good hormone. It is associated with feelings of euphoria, bliss, motivation, and concentration. Dopamine is released in the brain when something makes us feel good. Exercising, getting a massage, listening to music we enjoy, and spending quiet time with God, are just some of the ways to increase dopamine levels. Unfortunately, when life gets to be overwhelming, our adult children may turn to a device, instead of a person, for comfort and direction.

In my consulting practice I work with businesses that are ready to make some necessary changes: the kind that will result in a work environment and culture where the younger workforce can succeed. Shifting the business owner's mindset to one of taking responsibility, as well as the lead role in teaching social skills, communication skills, relationship building and sharing the benefits of perseverance and long-term effort to a specific end, to young adults, is no easy job. There is a need for clear direction, clear business models and consistent behaviors from businesses and corporations, for young adults to emulate.

Personal Prescription

As parents we want our adult children to work in environments that foster growth, inclusion, and consistently contribute to an employee's sense of value and well-being. If you are a business owner or you work for a business where it is clear that the younger adults employed seem less engaged, or there is consistent turnover among the younger adults, perhaps there is an opportunity for change. Change starts with sharing thoughts and exchanging ideas amongst like-minded professionals, and change can be executed with the help of a professional. If a business is growing, it should be changing with the ever-evolving landscape and demands of its clients, in order to remain relevant. There is tremendous benefit to keeping the younger adults employed. As a business owner myself, I want the fresh, energetic, creative and innovative ideas to continue to flow throughout my company. Consider moving in that direction, if you haven't already started, and try not to leave God out. It could be the prescription that takes you and your company to the next level.

Chapter 12:

Changing Roles

———— ● ● ————

*"If you could only love enough, you could be
the most powerful person in the world."*
EMMET FOX

I met a woman in the airport on my way home from
Washington DC. She and I hit it off right away. Our
kinship was formed when it was clear we had similar views
regarding the incredible rudeness of a fellow passenger.
We chose to sit next to each other on the plane, and ended
up talking together during the entire trip. I enjoyed every
moment of getting to know this amazing mother of three
adult children. She had lost a son just two years prior, to a
very unfortunate accident. She was not only still grieving,
but dealing with resentment from her other two children for
having asked them, earlier in the year, to leave her home. She
shared her belief that if she hadn't "kicked them out", as she
put it, they would continue to live off her and her husband,
with no end in sight. She spoke of her adult children with
love and admiration, and realized that she wasn't helping
them by allowing them to do the minimum to get by in life.
The last part of our conversation was all about the changing
roles parents play in the lives of their children.

When our children come into the world we move mountains as their nurturers and protectors. We then move steadily and transition into whatever the next phase of development is for our children, and into the role that corresponds with it…provider, educator, team coach, advocate, relationship coach, career coach, business coach, financial advisor, and friend. When our children become adults, the name of the game seems to be GIVE - Give Individuals Virtually Everything! We give advice. We give money. We give food. We give stuff. We give time. REPEAT. We give advice. We give money. We give food. We give stuff. We give time. REPEAT. We give love, of course. We wouldn't have it any other way.

I have friends who do some very interesting things to manage the impact of their adult children's behavior. Some put locks on their refrigerator and pantry doors. One couple even sold their home and downsized to an abode that could only accommodate the two of them. Staging, selling and packing up the family home gave the adult children a good eight months to get it together and make plans for themselves. The adult children ended up getting an apartment and moving in together. In a recent update, I've learned that the two young men are doing well…paying their rent and other bills on time, feeding themselves, and aspiring towards their goal of homeownership. Who knew! Well, just because I'm sharing this information doesn't mean that I advocate for selling your home and downsizing. Nor do I advocate for any of the other extremes some parents go through in order to accommodate their adult children. Nobody knows our children the way we do. You know what is best for your adult children, and even if you don't, you certainly know what is best for YOU.

Emerging adults need a different kind of closeness than when they were young. They need emotional support that helps boost, not stifle, their confidence in their own coping skills. They need parents to bear witness to their increasing capacity, regardless of how slow, to take on responsibilities, even if there are setbacks or mishaps along the way.

This is a perfect time to touch on the matter of our adult children becoming our friends. The timing of this relational shift is important to a healthy, functional relationship between parent and adult child. When your child reaches their twenties, you have choices to make about how much time to spend together; what type and how much information you feel they are ready for you to share with them; what battles are worth fighting; when to turn the other cheek and when to simply stay quiet, despite how strongly you feel about a particular thing. Regardless of age, we should always strive to be our child's best parent, so that when the timing is right, the transition to becoming their best or most trusted friend, can be natural and organic. The challenges in friendships between parents and their adult children come along when the parents cross those fine lines. Those times when you offer advice your child didn't ask for, or when you advocate for them when they were planning to handle or take care of a particular situation themselves. How about when you remind them to do that basic adult thing they already know is important to get done? You can imagine that sometimes we, unintentionally complicate matters and make things more challenging because of our own conditioning.

Now, let's continue to keep it real, you've got to know that not all adult children care to have their parents as friends, no less best friends. I have no idea what the future holds for me and my adult children, but today I feel quite certain that with all of the learning, listening, forgiving, healing and loving, we are in a good place for healthy friendships for the rest of our time here on earth. I'm claiming it! There are some things we can do to help condition our new relationships in a healthy way: (1) establish respectful boundaries - we want our adult children to respect us, our household, and the changes we go through as we age; especially our lack of tolerance for certain things. Doing the same for them will go a long way to increase respect and build confidence in our adult children; (2) we have got to listen more than we talk - offering unwelcome advice and asking too many questions that your young adult will undoubtedly consider as being nosy, will cause more harm than good. We have to bite our tongues and allow our adult children to continue to develop their own problem-solving and life skills; (3) carve out time to do the things you enjoy together - it's harder to find that balance when your children become adults, even when they are living at home. If your adult child has failed to launch, you may not have a desire to do fun things with them. You'd rather see them get off the coach and do something meaningful towards a goal of some sort. Guess what? Spending time with you, doing something you both enjoy, is incredibly meaningful in so many ways. I'll come back to this. I don't want to lose my train of thought here; (4) establish some rules for engagement for yourself - your adult child, regardless of their current challenges, or failure to launch, has their own ideas, opinions, principles, points of view, and values that may be different from yours. They also have developed some communication skills and judgement that can make it easier for them to see different perspectives. When there are times when it seems like a conflict will escalate, try to listen without interrupting, and then respond or comment in a neutral tone. If that doesn't work, you can always suggest taking a break and coming back to the topic when you both have calmed down; (5) lastly, make room for the special people in your adult children's lives - I can tell you that this was a hard one for me. We all want our children to pick the boyfriend or girlfriend who is smart, has common sense, and has positive things going for them. When my oldest daughter began dating, it seemed like it was her primary goal to choose the boy who had the very opposite of what my husband and I had hoped for. Just know that when your adult child makes the decision to settle on a partner, it will be natural for them to make that person the primary focus in their life. I bet that's what you did when you settled on a partner. I know I did, and I gave no thought to the impact it had on my parents.

So, I do want to go back to number three in the last paragraph. Even though it may not seem like it now, your young adult will someday be out of your home and living on their own. Finding time to do things with them will become harder as their lives improve, and other people come into their lives and take priority. Making a point of doing special things together now, even during times of stress and transition, can take the edge off the challenging dynamics at home. You are creating a necessary distraction, creating new and wonderful memories, as well as reminding your adult child that you love them, despite the current situation;

despite their choices. Remember the days of their youth when their greatest desire was to make you proud? You would be amazed at how a gesture like a simple invitation to do something you know you and your adult child would enjoy, can turn things around. We all want to be loved; our children especially need to know that we love them. What we do sometimes speaks louder than the words we say, and the attitude we emit. Scripture verses Romans 8:38-39 state: "For I am convinced that neither death nor life, neither angels nor demons, neither the present nor the future, nor any powers, neither height nor depth, nor anything else in all creation, will be able to separate us from the love of God that is in Christ Jesus our Lord." Imagine if we could come close to creating, in our adult children, a feeling of confidence in our love for them, the way God has done for us. Powerful!

When my son left our home to attend college in another state, I couldn't stop fretting over the thought that he would go away, get immersed in college life, and not call me at all. All I wanted was a call, at least once a week. You know, just to hear his voice and to make sure all was well with him. I knew that asking for any more than that would be met with resistance. At least that's what friends who walked the road before me said about their sons who went off to college. They said, "sons are very different from daughters." I fretted and fretted because my son was not a very communicative person. It wasn't in his nature to share much, and it took quite a bit of prying and nudging to get a conversation going with him. Well, to my pleasant surprise, and an overwhelming feeling of being blessed, my son called me regularly during his years of college. He kept in touch and kept me informed of his activities, adventures, accolades, and life lessons…even the difficult ones. It was godsend for me. I worried less and had a sense that when life threw the really big stuff his way, he would call me and use me as a resource and a guide. I'm sharing this because if I was a betting woman, I would have lost a ton on this one. No one could have convinced me that my son would have picked up the phone to talk; to get my thoughts and perspective on things. I want you to know that anything is possible. Actually, Matthew 19:26 states "…with God all things are possible."

We've already talked about all the wonderful things we want for our adult children and what we want them to grow to be…self-sufficient, successful, good-natured, possessing critical thinking and problem-solving skills. Well, I don't know about you, but I also want my adult children to have faith and a relationship with God. This is one of the roles I didn't mention earlier because I wanted to spend a little more time here. Have you ever said to yourself, especially in the aftermath of a challenging situation, "how do people manage and get through life's trials and tribulations without God?" I wonder this quite often. He's everything…forgiver of sins, healer, provider, counselor, refuge in times of trouble, master orchestrator, and the power by which things are done. I want my children to have Him for themselves; the access to everything they need to navigate this life here in the world. I hope my children will someday see me as someone they can trust to share truth and spiritual wisdom. I would be honored to fill the role of spiritual coach, if ever they are so inclined. I don't know everything, and while I can quote some scripture, I don't always know where in the Bible the verses are located. Although God is still doing a work in me, I'm no longer a babe in Christ who still feeds on milk.

I'm a mature Christian; a meat-eater who is a praying wife, mother, and grandmother.

If you think about it, as parents, we're actually in the business of putting ourselves out of a job when our children grow up, so nurture your own dreams while continuing to cultivate a close friendship with them. It makes for a wonderful, rich and meaningful life for all.

Personal Prescription

Be the one to take the first step in cultivating the friendship between you and your adult child. Consider reserving some time to make arrangements for the two of you to do that special thing you haven't done together in quite some time. It doesn't have to be long, a big deal or expensive. If there's a new, much-anticipated movie coming out, consider getting tickets for the two of you to go together. No talking; just the two of you enjoying the movie side by side. On the way to the movie, you talk only about the movie, and when it's over, you talk only about the movie on the ride home. Done! I mean it! You get home. Your child says thank you. You say "you're welcome", and you resist the urge to launch a "meaningful" conversation. The day for that will come.

Reflective and Ready

Chapter 13:

Girded for Success

––●—●––

"If you focus on success, you'll have stress. But if you pursue excellence, success will be guaranteed."

DEEPAK CHOPRA

I remember in my early days of working in corporate America that I was the only female in the board room. No one who sat at the table looked like me. That big, long, mahogany table surrounded by the tall back, plush, leather swivel chairs made for quite an impressive scene. I won't say that I was thrust into my job as leader of the tri-state support group, but I was expected to be incredibly more impressive than the furniture and the room it all sat in. Ha. Fortunately, everything I learned and experienced during my college and military years prepared me for a seat at the table. I was groomed and girded for success. What do I mean by girded, and what's the difference between that and being groomed? Being groomed means you are receiving help and support to learn, and improve upon, the skills or talents you will need to be successful in whatever your endeavor is. For me, being girded means that I am equipped as well as prepared. I possess what is necessary, whether that be experience, skills, or a toolbox full of tools for whatever the task or job at hand.

So, let's get in the zone, or a state of flow. For you, that may mean getting super focused or something else. For me, it's all about the space I'm in – my headspace and my physical space. An environment that fosters easy, flowing creativity. There's an energy that allows me to be in a good place to be open and ready to receive. Once we're there, and all feels right with the world, we can take inventory of how equipped we are to do what needs to be done. How prepared are we? Do we have what we need? Do we even know what we need? If we do know, how do we get it?

If we start with a current, most pressing need, what would it look like to help our adult children take the steps they need to become self-sufficient financially? I know several grown folks in their 40s and 50s who can pay their bills, but not able to make it completely on their own without the help of a spouse, other family members or friends. Some make the mistake of managing their finances with credit cards. Becoming financially self-sufficient requires taking steps to create a stable income, building savings, and staying out of significant debt. Living within one's means and having a healthy relationship with money is a key factor. We need a plan that we can propose to our adult child. A plan that speaks to their personality, talents, and gifts. Of course your child has talents and gifts. They just haven't felt the need to demonstrate them lately. This plan is all about generating revenue. Please, please, please.

This is not the "You need to get a job talk." My oldest daughter is an amazing cook. Her dishes are flavorful and yummy. She spends quite a bit of time in the kitchen and positions herself in front of the stove or oven when guests come to the house. She is the first to ask if anyone would like something to eat. She caters to everyone's needs and clearly feels satisfaction when people are enjoying her dishes and desserts. Everything is healthy, made from scratch with quality ingredients. Her lemon rounds are my personal favorite. After my own self-exploration, it came to me that something in the food catering industry might be of interest to my daughter. Before I'd share too much of my thinking, I simply asked her if she would be willing to cater a small reception for me. Words can't describe how she lit up at the idea. Well, let me try. If you've ever seen the Disney movie called Monsters, Inc., there's a scene at the very end when Sully opens the door to Boo's bedroom door and his face lights up like you wouldn't believe. My daughter's face lit up just like that. Well, that was the start. Man-oh-man was she in her element! She asked all the right questions, planned the menu, created her shopping list, and voila! My guests would be in store for a wonderful, tasty experience. The beginning of the unfolding of a money-generating plan. It was always the plan to pay my daughter for that gig, and from that, she would be doing other small events for some of my guests. A start is a start, and it's always a blessing when you can work and live in a way that celebrates your gifts.

Next, we could use some listening ears. It sounds like an elementary school thing, but most adults don't use theirs as much as they should, and today, everyone's attention span is short to a fault. If we are asking the universe about how we can help our adult children with opportunities that could help them progress and make positive changes, if we are truly listening, answers will start to pour in. Once the idea about food catering came to mind, my ears perk up every time someone needs an assistant at an event. I didn't hear any of this before the idea came into my spirit. I assure you. I may have heard the words, but I didn't have on my listening ears. I've even taken it a step further. I ask people who are hosting events if they could use an extra set of hands. What's better than doing the very thing you love and are truly gifted at. Who knew!

Another important element is how we use our time. I'm not talking about classic, buzz-phrase "time management skills." I'm talking about being a good steward of the time we have with our adult children during their "paralyzed-by-God-only-knows what" phase. They are living in your home. Did you know that in exchange for them being able to flick the light switch and get light, them being able to turn on the faucet and get water, and them being able to open the fridge and get food, that you can ask certain things in return? This is not meant to be sarcastic, and while rent money and help with groceries would be wonderful, quality time in working together toward mastery in something has a great deal of value. So, here's what we work toward in the Reid house – mastery in how we use our day. Why? Because how you start and use your day absolutely matters! I'm not asking everyone to get up as insanely early as I do, or to start some boring routine, but I do want to share the importance of doing something physical every single day; that praying and sitting still long enough to be reflective is important; that intentionally seeking out and learning something new each and every day is a stimulating part of the journey; operating within your gifts is essential to being a true expression of yourself; and that spending just a little time prioritizing the order of things planned for your day helps to ensure that the important things get done. It looks different for each of us. I complete four of these things before 7 a.m. Yep, done by 7 a.m. It's the only way I know how to have incredibly efficient and productive days. I just realized how often I use the word incredibly. I didn't realize until just now how much I must like the word. Webster says it means: "To a great degree; extremely or unusually." I guess I use it for effect. Is it working?

Sorry, where was I? Right, so it's a thing in my house to celebrate each other's successes. We share lots of stories during meal times. Yes, we have meals together whenever our schedules permit, and we try to do this more often than not. I know that each of us looks forward to these family discussions and storytelling, and just so you know, we laugh a lot as we listen to our stories. We especially laugh at ourselves. I do however, pray that one day they'll come to learn that they can each drastically change their life by starting the day earlier. Much earlier – a little at a time.

So, who do your adult children choose to surround themselves with? Who do they have in their ear? Who's giving them advice? Who's setting examples for them to follow? I hope it's not other adult children who have failed to launch. Everyone needs support and encouragement at times. We especially need the truth. When we are not doing the right thing, perhaps we've lost sight of what's really going on in a certain situation, or maybe we just don't recognize how we've contributed to it. An honest, tell-it-like-it-is friend is a real gem. We can't always be that for our adult children, but we can be wise and discerning about who we allow into our homes to spend time with our families.

That said, who's on board with you as you embark upon this endeavor to turn things around in a positive way? Your spouse? Your significant other? A dear friend? Whoever it is, there's a way to engage them so they will be an active participant in the endeavor. First off, we can't ever assume that our loved one is experiencing our present life circumstances the same way we are. The likelihood is that we are not. The same way I considered my adult child and what would resonate most with her, you can do the same when considering how to engage your loved one. This is very important because you're going to need the support. It's integral to your success for you and your partner to be seen and heard by your adult children, as unified.

Being seen. You know you always have the option and ability to visualize yourself, your adult children and your spouse in a dynamic that best mirrors what you've always hoped and dreamed it would be. Visualization is a tool that has powerful applications in personal and professional development, and transformation. Seeing, consistently visualizing your desired outcome as it makes its way to manifestation, is incredibly powerful.

There are countless tools in the coaching and consulting world that I can add to your current, working toolbox. Better yet, I'd love to have the opportunity to add them to your repertoire. Perhaps one day soon we'll find a common ground and work together beyond this book. In the meantime, let me suggest this one last thing for the tool belt you'll have girded around your waist. When you feel exhausted, exasperated, and about to explode, try to keep in mind that when you are feeling this way, you are more likely to be easily triggered by the next exhausting and irritating event or situation. Exercise your right to choose and try to separate yourself – for however long it takes to get back to being grounded in a spirit of gratitude. It will fare you incredibly well, and everyone else who comes into contact with you. What's worse than a hothead? Two hotheads, I bet! It's not an easy cycle to stop, but the one thing that works best for me is to go through my mental Rolodex of people and things to be thankful for, reminding myself about how much God loves me. From there, I am better able to shift my thinking from what someone else is doing, to the root cause of why someone is doing whatever they are doing.

When I first moved to Georgia, I spent the first six years in training to become a black belt in Tae Kwon Do. I have lots of fond memories about my years at the Tae Kwon Do Center in Hampton, Georgia, but the one thing that always surfaces in my mind, especially when I am in conflict, is the little nugget of profound wisdom our instructor bestowed upon us. He told us to remember that no matter how bad things get, no matter how ugly someone is to you, always be a pretty flower. He said this to the whole class, not just to the women. Think about it. What a wonderful way to distinguish yourself in the midst of adversity or turmoil. Be a pretty flower – one that I imagine smells just as beautiful as it looks. Kee-yah!

Personal Prescription

When you invest in yourself, you invest in your future. One of the important ways you can prepare yourself for success in anything is to take time for yourself. At the start of your day, take time to disconnect from the world – no cell phone, no television, and no computer. Sit still, calm your body, and close your eyes. Center yourself in a way so that when your mind wanders, you can acknowledge the wandering but keep working on settling yourself back to the present moment. Begin to ask yourself questions about what you want in your life. Please be sure you answer these questions with positive words, images, and feelings about the new you. If your past self-wanders into this experience, acknowledge it, and go directly back to the words, images, and feelings about the new you; the relationships the new you has, the new role the new you has, and whatever else is positive for your future self. Do this every day. You will be amazed at the positive changes that will occur in your life.

Chapter 14:

Casting Shade

———•—•———

"You can't be friends with someone who wants your life."
OPRAH WINFREY

I love listening to and talking to millennials. They are such a different, amazing, and interesting brood. I found myself sharing the details of a situation at work with my two adult children. I followed the story with how I planned to celebrate the person who was emanating so much negativity toward me. My daughter responded in the way she always does: questioning why I insist on doing nice things for not-so-nice people. My son, on the other hand, responded with an explanation about what people do when they are jealous or just miserable. He used the term casting shade. He shared that it's typical for some people who don't want to see you do well. They don't even want to see other people compliment you or celebrate you in some way, so they cast shade on your sunshine.

How many of you have people in your life who cast shade? It could be the family member who never seems to support anything you do or say. They're the ones who always find ways to poke holes in your ideas. Perhaps it's someone at work or someone in your community who just can't help bringing and speaking negativity when you come around. The worst is the person or group of people who cast shade on you but do it behind your back. This is sad and unfortunate, but very common. Well, let me just say that as much as there will always be opportunities for you to shine, there will be equal opportunities for folks to cast shade. So, if we know it, we can prepare for it. That doesn't mean we focus on it or give it energy. We are just simply aware, and we decide in advance that it will not become a barrier to the wonderful things God is doing in our lives.

Remember that when light exists, darkness cannot prevail. 1 John 2:9 says, "Anyone who claims to be in the light but hates a brother or sister is still in the darkness." Hate, jealousy, you name it. Know that not everyone has your best interest at heart, that some people have a negative and inaccurate viewpoint and will posture themselves in a way to try to become obstacles to your new and exciting life. Some folks can't help it. They have their own issues they have yet to address and resolve. Oftentimes, they haven't been self-reflective enough to even recognize that there is something, some aspect of their life, that needs love and attention.

OK, so we recognize people can become obstacles, especially when you compare yourself to them! It's so easy to fall into this trap and it's the quickest way to thinking you're not good enough or you don't deserve this or that. Good enough for what? Good enough for everything you've been dreaming and praying about. Success for your adult children. A supportive spouse. Starting your new business. Engaging in your community in a significant way, and the list goes on. How about instead we meditate on the fact that our gifts are unique to each of us and that no one can be or do either of us as well as we can. Love it! Also, let's not pay too much attention to what others think. Decide in advance what matters more to you – the approval of other people or expressing yourself fully and living your best life?

What about the things you perceive as obstacles? The negative things and scenarios that churn around in your mind are the very things that can paralyze you. Let's go back to the Barriers Have Names exercise. Let's ask the universe what we need to do to remove these barriers or change them into breakthroughs. We have to ask because the answer is different for each of us. Is there a need to make a tough decision? Is the answer simply to acknowledge that the barrier exists? Is it a matter of having a conversation with someone? Is it time to remove or add something? Let's pray and ask.

So, life happens – to all of us. You know how when the weatherman predicts the arrival of a storm, you usually have some time to prepare for it. You can purchase some extra groceries, stock up on batteries and candles, and whatever you need. When life's storms come our way, however, we are often blindsided and find ourselves overwhelmed. Life's storms can often cause delays, but I believe wholeheartedly that delays have a purpose. It could be that there is something else you need to learn, something else you need to obtain, and someone else you need to meet and connect with, something else you need to experience before your dream is manifested. I don't know. I'm not a prophet but I do believe that everything happens for a reason. Romans 8:28 says, "And we know that in all things God works for the good of those who love him, who have been called according to his purpose." Try not to be disappointed in delays. They could be a significant factor in reaching your destiny. You can't really prepare for life's unexpected challenges, but you can have faith that you will get through them. In my personal experience, there are times when I'm about to embark upon something new and wonderful; something may come along to try to keep me from experiencing it or making progress. You may be derailed physically, but you don't have to be derailed mentally. Remember the big rig story, right?

Everything, and I do mean everything, begins with a thought. We don't always have control of whether these thoughts are positive or negative. You know how often the negative ones slip in, but we can practice replacing negative thoughts with positive ones, and we can focus on what the Bible tells us to do in 2 Corinthians 10:5, "We demolish arguments and every pretension that sets itself up against the knowledge of God, and we take captive every thought to make it obedient to Christ." This is from the English Standard Version, the version my late Aunt Eva used. I promise you that this is something you can become better and better at with practice. I know first-hand that the life I am living today is the sum total of the thoughts I've been thinking up to this point. Yes. I believe that. I also believe that energy flows where attention goes. What you focus on grows. Whatever is the focus of attention manifests and becomes more prominent in your life.

Why do I believe this? It's exactly what has been the case for me my entire adult life. I've always been confident about being successful. I've always believed I would travel. I've always believed that goodness and mercy will follow me all the days of my life. I know, right? Good and mercy? Here's why. When I was a child, my Aunt Eva, God rest her soul, sang Psalm 23:6 to me every day whenever we were together; every single day. I found myself singing the words to this scripture well into high school, through my military days, through my corporate days, and, to this very day, I sing it in the quiet of the night to rest my soul, and to my new grandson! When I mentioned Kye earlier, did I mention how stinkin' cute he is? Sorry. I digress again. Something as simple and powerful as having a disciplined thought life can sometimes be too obvious for people to fully grasp and consistently apply. I'm certainly not perfect. I waiver and have to remind myself on occasion how important it is to capture any thought that rears itself up against God's promises and the plans He has for me.

Let's consider another obstacle. It's the filter you have and use when you give and receive information. It's the filter that determines how you receive messages and experience people. It's when you're in a meeting with someone who is not very nice, and you know has ill-intent. Let's go back to my neighbor from Chapter 5. She not only has a reputation in the community for being less than kind, she has shown me her true self on more than one occasion. You can imagine that the filter by which I listen to her or engage with her might be a little clogged, right? I want to protect myself, my feelings. Who openly wants to be hurt, disrespected, or brought down? Not anyone that I know. So, we do have to consider our filters. How did I do it that day standing at the threshold of my garage? How did I say those genuine words of congratulations and best wishes? I reminded myself that God is love and that I had to see my neighbor through God's lenses. I reminded myself of how blessed I am and that my cup runneth over. A flood of gratitude sweeps over me when I think these thoughts and remind myself of whom God is in me. It makes it much easier to respond to others in love. This would be a good time to go back to your FLOW worksheet. Because I'm not perfect, I find myself asking for forgiveness, more often than I'd like, just like you.

Some people, not you or I, are all talk and no action. They talk for years about a different life, a different situation, even a different person. Year after year, they talk about the same things and never really put any practical things into action. It can be exhausting. Sometimes we just have to get out of our own way, push our fears and the attitude and beliefs of others to the side. I know it's easier said than done, so just practice. Do something different, shake things up a bit and surprise yourself even. You do this enough and, before you know it, you'll be able to see and experience first-hand how you can recondition your mind and transform your life.

Remember the term "scaredy cat" from your childhood? It meant that you were a timid person; that you were afraid of something. Were you ever called a scaredy cat? How about being called "chicken" followed by "puk puk pukaaak!" Being "chicken" meant the same thing. Did either of these names get you going? Get you to a place where you wanted to prove the kid on the playground wrong? Tell me, because if it did, and calling you a scaredy cat or a yellow-bellied chicken will evoke enough emotion in you to cause you to move, take action, and do something different, I'll do it! OK, just trying to be a little light-hearted here. I know this is serious stuff. I know we've been the way we are for a super long time, and I know we are the way we are because of something or someone, right? No, not really. Remember, we are not victims, we are victors, and we've been working hard.

Looking at ourselves when we've found others to blame for so long is hard work.

I love the you you're becoming. Soon you won't even recognize yourself. You'll be like, wait, did I just say that? Did I really just do that? It's going to feel like a breath of fresh air to be so less uptight and conditioned in a specific way. The energy around you will flow like a refreshing breeze on a Georgia summer day; not just refreshing to you but to everyone who comes in contact with you. Keep your eyes open for opportunities to add color to your life. We can all find ourselves exacerbated by our own situation and circumstances, and when this happens, we don't want this feeling to last longer than is healthy for us to feel it. Get out and try a new place to eat; switch up your exercise regimen; splurge on a little something new for yourself. Celebrate often.

You, your family, your friends, your whomever else you're close to, have each other and that's huge. Rearrange things so they feel included and engage them in a way that gives them insight into the new you. If anyone starts casting shade, you know what to do.

Personal Prescription

When it comes to people casting shade, being negative and judgmental, folks will often suggest that you just simply not associate yourself with people like this, or simply remove them from your life. But what do you do when the people casting shade are family members or people you work with or serve with every day? Not so simple then. My suggestion would be to use the negative energy people like this emanate for your own character development. You don't need to get sucked into their pool of pessimism. You don't need to get pierced every time they try to poke at you. We become better people when we understand that everyone has a story. We have no idea why people behave the way they do; what their negative behavior is rooted in, and despite how they treat us, or how they try to make us feel, we can choose to offer love and compassion in every situation. No, it's not easy, but I can tell you first-hand that it's the best option. You rise above the negativity, and if we are really in charge of our own emotions, we can stay centered, grounded, peaceful, and calm, when the naysayers and haters try to bring us down.

Chapter 15:

Cheering from the Sidelines

———●●———

"While God is working on your problem... stay calm, stay sweet, stay out of fear, and keep on keepin' on."
JOYCE MEYER

I believe it was a weekday in 1989 when I was riding the New York City subway on my way to work. Out of nowhere my nostrils began to fill with a terrible stench; the kind of smell that instantly makes you nauseous. It was early on a rush-hour morning and the passengers were packed on the subway like sardines. As was normal when folks are squeezing onto the train, bodies were touching but no one is making eye contact with anyone. When the combined smell of urine, vomit, and feces hit my nose, I looked up to follow the stench and see that the others around me are doing the same.

A homeless person had managed to squeeze himself onto the train, and believe it or not, as packed as the train is, the passengers next to the homeless person were safe, at least for the time being. Without words or communication of any kind, the passengers had decided it was OK to be practically on top of each other. No one wanted to make contact with this person. There was literally an empty horse-shoe-shaped space about a foot wide around the homeless person.

Once he had everyone's attention, he began, with a loud, clear voice, to ask each of us about why we were willingly heading to a place we really don't want to go to, to spend the entire day with people we really don't even like. He wanted to know why we do this every day of the week, and why we choose not to spend just as much time with the people we love. He continued with asking why we always buy flowers for the people we love and care about when they are dead, instead of buying them flowers while they are alive. He finished with stating that our loved ones might appreciate and enjoy the flowers if they received them while they are alive.

There was complete silence in the subway car as the passengers, myself included, contemplated this man's words. The train stopped at Penn Station less than a minute after his speech, and we were all relieved to exit the train – incredibly so. I don't know how many of the passengers who were in that particular train car that day thought any more about what the man said, I just know that I did – and still do. I share his sentiment with folks whenever the right opportunity presents itself. It's important to take regular stock in what you're doing with your life. Are you doing the things you are supposed to be doing? Are you doing meaningful work? Do you have proper balance in your life? Are you living your life in the way you want to or the way someone else expects you to? Are you spending enough time doing the things you enjoy? Have you asked the universe how you can grow further? How you can make a difference in the lives of others? This is an important exercise. The years are not standing still my friend. They are moving along. Are you? Being stuck and in some sort of bondage is not a good or healthy place to be.

"To give anything less than your best is to sacrifice the gift." This is a quote by Steve Prefontaine, the American runner and Olympiad. I would go as far as to say, "To give anything less than your absolute best is to sacrifice the gift." There's a downside to doing nothing when there's so much you can do, and when there's so much at stake. Doing nothing suggests that we accept our current situation for what it is. Accepting a mediocre life is not an option here; neither is giving up on your adult child, your spouse, or your dreams. There's also a downside to giving less than your best. You've heard this before: What you put into something is what you'll get out of it. You want more? Do more. You want better. Do better. No, it's not as plain and as simple as that. I know and understand that all too well; especially when it seems like you're the only one who wants "more" and "better." Remember the quote by Frederick Douglass I shared? "The collapse of character begins with compromise." Let's make a pact right now not to compromise when it comes to our families, our businesses, or our dreams. Let's add to this pact that we will enlist an accountability partner whenever necessary. There's such value in having one. First and foremost, they can be one of your biggest cheerleaders, always motivating you with the "You can do it" attitude and positive energy to accompany it. It's incredibly helpful to know that someone is in your corner, ready when necessary, to remind you of your goals and dreams, and most importantly, the why behind them. You certainly won't feel alone with an accountability partner, especially on the days that are tougher than others.

One of my clients shared with me an amazing idea for an invention. This idea will significantly change the way we entertain today. I listened intently and with joy in my heart, as the story of her plan unfolded. We must have bounced ideas off one another and with so much energy, for at least an hour. My client shared how supported she felt, and I shared with her what an honor it was for me to be someone she felt safe enough to share her idea with. She knows me well enough at this stage in our relationship that I will cheer for her from the sidelines. I will encourage her, share information with her that is relevant to her idea, and whenever I can, connect her to individuals that can help bring her project to fruition. These are the things cheerleaders do, and the term "sidelines" doesn't mean distant or absent. It means that I'm right there, watching and seeing where and how I can play a part, all while celebrating the idea as if it's already manifested. When some of the supplies for the project arrived at her home, we got even more excited. It's the little things you have to celebrate along the way. It's important. It keeps the excitement and the momentum going.

During one of our sessions, I felt like my client's energy and enthusiasm for her idea was on the verge of being sabotaged by the all-too-familiar fear and anxiety sisters. You can refer to them as brothers or cousins if you'd like. The two of them often go hand-in-hand; one is not typically felt without the other. I listened, and when she gave me an opportunity, I shared the downside of her not seeing this project to the end. Since her idea had everything to do with entertainment and her home, I told her that she would more than likely feel a hint of conviction every time she looked at a particular item or entertained in her home. She would feel regret and sadness for the idea she didn't birth. The absence of her product would be a source of contention every time she was preparing to use the item or have guests over. The thought of that was plenty enough to get my client back on track. She acknowledged that she feels enough conviction and regret every time her New Year's resolutions go by the wayside, when she falls off a diet, yet again, or when she doesn't honor a commitment she's made to someone. These were feelings she'd like to avoid if she could.

My wish for you and yours is simply that you achieve your goals and that your dreams come true. It doesn't happen magically though. You've got to do something and play the starring role. Imagine if we protected our dreams like we do our loved ones. Seriously. We'd nurture them and give them the attention they deserve. We'd never intentionally lose them or ignore them. We'd try our darnedest to make sure they blossomed and reached their full expression. People say there is no instruction book on how to live but I would argue that oh yes there is. Maybe not the way you'd think of one in a traditional hardcover, instruction book or an e-book. This instruction comes by way of people and circumstances, trials, and tribulations. You've got to condition yourself to be aware, to be open, and to be receptive. The universe is always communicating with you.

Today I have new lenses, and the prescription for them did not appear overnight. It has been a process in the making for some time now. I will say that the prescription has been in the refining stage for the past five years – all that I've learned, all that I've experienced, and all that I've taken for granted. And like most prescriptions, at some point, I'll need a new one. It's one thing to intellectualize a concept; something new. It's another for it to resonate and for you to put the learning into reasonable practice.

I don't know how you feel about the statement, "The fruit doesn't fall far from the tree," but it's always been a tough one for me. It suggests that a child has a similar character and similar qualities to his or her parents. I've had people tell me with a great deal of confidence that they know my oldest daughter is doing great. "Just look at her, momma!" I would just smile and feel the weight of the truth. With my new lenses, I no longer have a heavy heart. I understand that the universe will respond to my adult child, as the universe will also respond to me. My daughter's life is her own. She is an adult who has free will to make choices, to make mistakes, to make resolutions, to make amends, or to make it up as she goes. My role as a parent is not to perpetuate any behavior that is not in her best interest or that will not lead to the best version of her. My role is not to be an enabler. Being an enabler can be just as harmful to me, as it is to her. My role, at least as I believe, is to be the best role model I can be, to be creative and understanding in my attempts to help her navigate through this life. To love her – unconditionally.

Today, my oldest daughter is a mother and looking forward to starting a new career. She gave birth to the cutest baby ever. I mean the most incredible baby ever. Oh, don't mind me. Having my first grandchild is the very thing that has my cup running over with blessings. My daughter is thrilled to be a mother but is coming to terms very quickly with the fact that going from no children to being responsible for just one child is one of the toughest transitions a woman can make. How do you adjust from sleeping in to waking up every 2-3 hours? How do you adjust to not being able to be spontaneous anymore with your time? Your goings and comings are now dictated by the needs of another human being. I'm cheering for her though. A crying baby, sleepless nights, and postpartum depression can take a toll on a new mom. I'm cheering for her too because she is amazing. I am looking forward to her realizing that about herself. She's a cutie too – freckles and all. As a mom, she'll find herself experiencing the deepest relationship imaginable, with her son. As a mom, she'll find herself dealing with many of the things I have dealt with in my life's walk, but what I hope she always overcomes is the feeling that her life's circumstances can be so overwhelming that her dreams are no longer a priority. I pray she gets and stays close to God. At least she knows for certain that her son has a praying grandmother.

Imagine if we could choose and control all the situations and circumstances in our life so that our "resting face," like our Bitmoji's and avatars, was always one of peace and happiness. Well, that would be incredibly awesome but you know we can't, so what can we do? What I did was recognize I need some new lenses, make some tough decisions, and then use the tools specifically designed to help me achieve the outcome I desire.

Just know that I'm cheering for you. I most certainly am. The way I do for my clients, my family and my friends. You have things to do that will impact others. I know without a shadow of a doubt that you were created to do something incredible; something unique to you. How do you define incredible? Whatever your definition, please know that I believe in you and that you've got me cheering for you from the sidelines.

Personal Prescription

I am excited to have another person to support and cheer for, but it's more important to me that you cheer for yourself. Affirm yourself and be your biggest cheerleader. Start to give thanks in advance for what's already yours – that thing, that transformation, that new plan, that new outlook, your new lenses! Make sure that as you affirm yourself, your list of "I am's" is nice and long and filled with all things positive. I am thankful. I am able. I am love. I am victorious. I am creative. I am charitable. I am a good steward. I am happy. I am positive. Don't ever criticize yourself. You deserve the same kindness you extend to others, and remember that every day, and I do mean every day, is yet another opportunity to pursue your goals and dreams. It's another chance to experience the richness that exists in all that God has given to you. You don't have to wait for the New Year, or the beginning of a new week, a new month, or new quarter. The 'day', whichever one you choose, is as good a day as any.

Acknowledgments

The idea for this book came from God.

I believe that the experiences and challenges God allows to take place in our lives are meant to grow, develop, and mature us.

The courage for this book came from God.

Fear and love cannot coexist. God is love and my ever-present help in times of need.

The completion of this book is due to God.

He put the right people, in the right place, at the right time, under the right circumstances, for this book to be completed and published.

I am truly blessed by my husband Craig, my daughters Kyli and Jessi, my son Tyree, and my one and only grandson Kye. I want to thank them for allowing me to give much of my time and service to others. I thank them for their love, their patience, and for forgiving me, every time I stumbled and fumbled. In the words of our very own Miss Jessi, "I love you more."

I want to acknowledge that I am well-aware, and feel constantly, the unconditional love that my brother, Mark Tyree, has for me. Everyone needs someone who's got their back - no matter what.

I am in awe of the incredible faith consistently demonstrated by one of my dearest friends, and Godmother to my son, Maria Segarra; whose life is a testament that prayer works and that love, does in fact, endure all.

I am incredibly grateful to my long-time friend, Tracy Skinner, whose honesty, sense of humor and constant affirmation in my abilities are a constant stream of love and support.

God has always placed incredibly amazing people in my life and along my path. The one and only MaDear, is one such loving spirit. Thank you for taking me in.

I must acknowledge the strength demonstrated by my sister, Desiree Kelske; an internal strength that can be an example to many, not only to me. While the fire is hot, and the journey has some painful twists and turns, I feel confident that you will come out unscathed and not smelling like smoke.

Lastly, I want to thank and acknowledge my sister-in-law Tiffany, and my mother-in-law Cynthia, for being genuine and sincere examples of love and forgiveness.

To the Morgan James Publishing team: Special thanks to David Hancock, CEO & Founder for believing in me and my message. To my Author Relations Manager, Tiffany Gibson, thanks for making the process seamless and easy. Many more thanks to everyone else, but especially Jim Howard, Bethany Marshall, and Nickcole Watkins.

About the Author

Pam Reid is the founder of FLOW (feel love over worry), and President of FLOW Consulting. Pam received her degree in Business Management while serving in the United States Air Force. Pam is an entrepreneur, professional speaker, business consultant and success coach.

Pam was born and raised in New York where she spent the majority of her corporate years working for Deloitte, a financial services firm. She led and managed the largest client service support group in the tri-state region and was deemed a subject-matter expert in client satisfaction, human resources, and professional development and training.

Throughout her career, Pam has spent many years working with parents and young adults, in their quest to become advocates, leaders, self-reliant, and self-aware. Her experiences include creating a parent leadership program, as well as student leadership, internship, and career development programs.

Pam is actively engaged in her community. She is a member of the Board of Directors for her local Chamber of Commerce. She is a Paul Harris Fellow Rotarian, and the Scholarship Chair for a local chapter of the American Business Women's Association.

Pam has had the pleasure and honor of gracing the cover of Fayette Woman magazine, and been the recipient of several community service and leadership awards. Pam is married to her high school sweetheart and together they have three children, and one new grandson! She is a black belt in Tae Kwan Do and loves to participate in annual sporting events. Pam is an avid reader who also enjoys photo journaling and traveling.

Thank You!

Thank you for reading *New Lenses*.

If you're due for a new prescription and you're genuinely ready for a set of new lenses, I'm here to help. It's one thing to want change and talk about change; it's quite another thing to take the first step, and to continue to walk through it!

To support you in your efforts, I'm offering a FREE 4-part video series – a $400 value – designed to be the ideal complement to *New Lenses*.

To receive access to this free video series, please email me at Pam@newlensesbookseries.com.

Oh, and here's a bonus! When you receive the free 4-part video series, we'll send you the Lenses Repair Kit – a $150 value absolutely free. With these foundational resources, you'll be well on your way to being equipped to see your journey through.

P.S. This is exciting! Please share your progress with me at Pam@newlensesbookseries.com. I'd love to hear from you.